W9-AOJ-238

The Workshop Way of Learning

The Workshop Way
of Learning

by

Earl C. Kelley

**Professor of Secondary Education,
Wayne University, Author of
"Education for What Is Real"**

Harper & Brothers · Publishers

NEW YORK

THE WORKSHOP WAY OF LEARNING

Copyright, 1951, by Harper & Brothers
Printed in the United States of America

K-A

To My Mother
Eliza Morley Kelley
teacher–poet–musician
this book is affectionately dedicated

Contents

Contents

Foreword

Man has been searching for a more effective method of putting into practice the truths that have become known about how people learn. It is vital that a way be found to establish an environment which enables children and adults to learn. This environment must bring about recognition of individual worth; and it must help us to learn how to live among our fellow men with more understanding. A way must be found to enable groups of people to learn from each other and help each other toward the solution of common problems. Wayne University is continually seeking better methods to meet these needs. We who have experienced the method of the Education Workshop are convinced that through it and other similar experiences these goals can be accomplished. We have found that the workshop creates changes in the individual that make him not only a better person and a more effective teacher, but a person whose relations with his students will be more wholesome and productive.

This book describes the method through which we experienced these things. It will be an aid to those who are preparing for such an experience for themselves as well as an aid to those who are planning to provide the experience for others. The book explains the method through which children can learn vastly more than through any other approach so far known to the problem of education. As students of Wayne University who have experienced this workshop and practiced its methods, we firmly believe the story of the workshop as described by Dr. Kelley will help those who are searching for a better way of learning. We also feel that the need for this book is critical, that if the American way of life is to survive, our society must be fortified with better educated citizens. We are grateful to

ix

Wayne University for providing this enriching experience, and
we wish to acknowledge the skillful leadership of the workshop staff.

ARTHUR H. BROWN
MORREL J. CLUTE
BETTY JEAN JONES
LAURA E. NEEF
FRANK J. PIES

Preface

The idea of writing this book, and the inspiration necessary to get me started, came to me during the spring conference at Waldenwoods in 1949. There I saw people working together when they might have been playing. I saw people being changed, so that from then on they would have to operate differently. And I came again to realize that it is only when we can devise experiences which change people that we can affect practice.

The conference was an experience in intensified human relations. People were not only learning from each other, but they were coming into close communion with other human beings. The walls that isolate behind which they had been living were being washed away, so that they no longer needed to "go it alone." Great revelation was coming to people who, in many cases, were for the first time gaining the fruit of commonalty with other humans. It is only by doing things with others toward commonly accepted goals that this commonalty can be gained, and the basic loneliness of the human spirit can be assuaged.

The workshop staff had been working together for nine years without having reduced our beliefs or our methods to writing. This task became one of stating what we believe and how we wanted to bring these beliefs into operation.

It seems to me that the book describes action research. We have our hypotheses, and the ways by which we attempt to verify them. It is research because we never know whether what we try is going to work or not. We have been in a continuous process of formulating and discarding. We hope the day will never come when we have *the* procedure which we think is the final answer. When unique human beings are involved, this finality is impossible. Unexamined methods in teaching have done much to routinize and stultify learning. There are many teachers today who have never once asked themselves what their real objectives are or whether or not their methods accomplish them. Teaching is the only trade or profession I can think of where the practitioner can go through an entire career without ever relating objectives, methods, and outcomes.

This is a book on method—on the "how." We seem to be coming into an era of method. There are signs all about the country that people are becoming interested at last in how we put beliefs into action. Most teachers and lay people can agree on wholesome objectives for education. Violent disagreement comes when we confront the question as to how these objectives are to be accomplished. Perhaps the era of "how" has to come soon because we have all given lip service to the tenets of democracy as long as we can without doing something about it.

There is also agreement in many places that skill in human relations is the most important learning one can experience. Whatever the learner may do or wherever he may go, we know that he will have to deal with other people. The only way by which human relations can be learned so that the learning will function and will modify behavior is by having experiences in working and playing with other people. We cannot teach a skill without having the learner try it.

These methods, modified to suit the occasions, can be used by all kinds of people, wherever people are gathered together to learn and the possibilities of human relationships are thereby intensified. It is only incidental that this experiment has been carried out with teachers.

The methods can be useful to industry. Large corporations have long had training programs for their employees, especially supervisors and foremen. Often these training programs have failed to increase the skill of the trainees in their most important responsibility, that of getting along with those with whom they must work.

Labor also has programs of education where the development of skills in human relations is needed. The methods can be useful in adult education, Parent-Teacher Associations, professional schools, and Arts colleges. They are universal to people, as learning is universal.

Some readers may criticize this book on the ground that it is full of obvious minutiae. This I feel to be true, but I have believed that the best way to write a book on method is to describe what we have done and found to work, carefully and in detail. This is a description of techniques involved and used. It is therefore not theoretical. Some of the little devices which seem so simple took us five years to learn. Perhaps the simple is that which one has already discovered, and the complex or profound is that which remains to be contrived.

It is obvious that I am indebted to many more people than I can mention here. I ought to list all the workshoppers and staff members for the past ten years. We could not have had this experience without the effort of other people in other places, who gave the workshop method its impetus. I will have to limit myself to the present staff, all of whom helped by reading and criticizing the manuscript. The book should and would have been written by the staff, except for difficulties involved in arranging the time for working together. They are Morris Better, industrial arts teacher at the Garfield Intermediate School, Detroit; Morrel Clute, counselor and social studies teacher at Rochester, Michigan; Roland C. Faunce, associate professor of secondary education, Wayne University; George L. Miller, director of admissions, Wayne University; Marie I. Rasey, professor of educational psychology, Wayne University; Collins J. Reynolds, social studies teacher at the Garfield Intermediate School, Detroit; and Rebecca Wignot, English teacher at Miller High School, Detroit. Mr. Clute and Mrs. Wignot were not on the staff at the same time, but both worked on the manuscript.

The foreword was written by a committee of present and former workshoppers. It is really a piece of composite writing, since they almost literally took turns in supplying words.

Arthur H. Brown teaches seventh grade in Dearborn, Michigan. Morrel J. Clute is a present staff member, as cited above. Betty Jean Jones teaches social studies in the River Rouge, Michigan Junior High School. Laura E. Neef is a mathematics teacher in the Barbour Intermediate School, Detroit. Frank J. Pies is pastor of the Salem Lutheran Church, Detroit, and principal of its parochial school.

I wish to express my special gratitude to Mrs. Julia Morgan Mason for her assistance.

E. C. K.

December 1, 1950

The Workshop Way of Learning

CHAPTER I
Introduction

This is the story of what has been going on during the last ten years in the Education Workshop at Wayne University. It is a story of dilemma, frustration, invention, and creation toward a better way of teaching and learning. It is a tale of the good will, enthusiasm, confidence, and courage of a thousand men and women—teachers seeking better ways to live with their children in school. It is a story of adventure on the growing edge of the learning process.

The Wayne University Education Workshop was started in 1938 by Dean Waldo E. Lessenger, of the College of Education, Wayne University, and Dr. John R. Emens, who is now president of Ball State Teachers College, Muncie, Indiana. Dr. Emens directed it for two years, when, in September of 1940, the writer took his place. It has, at this time (spring of 1951) operated without interruption for thirteen years, which is, so far as we know, a long-distance record for any workshop. What follows has to do only with the last ten years, since it is all written from first-hand experience.

The workshop operates from 4:30 P.M. to 9:00 P.M. on Thursdays throughout the academic year. Time is taken out for eating dinner together. This particular workshop has never operated in the summer session. Each semester is a workshop by itself, although students are permitted to receive credit for it for two semesters. Each semester we have some students who were with us the semester before, and some new ones. We usually have a few who have had two or more semesters of it, and are taking it without credit. The numbers have varied

1

from a low point of thirty-five (during the busiest time of the war) to one hundred and twenty. A typical postwar workshop usually has from ninety to one hundred teachers.

The workshop gives both graduate and undergraduate credit. It is open to experienced teachers, with no limitations as to grade levels or subjects taught. Recently some of our preservice teachers who are currently doing directed teaching have been coming into the workshop. This gives us a heterogeneous group with one thing in common—an interest in children and in the improvement of teaching methods.

In the early days of the workshop, we came face to face with the problem of what to do with a hundred teachers, a block of time, and freedom. What was the very best experience for teachers which we could create? What program would best send them back to their pupils Friday morning refreshed and with renewed faith and courage to face the day? What habits and clichés of college teaching could we dispense with, and what offerings would stimulate creativeness?

This book is written in an effort to tell what we have done about these questions. When did the scales begin to fall from our eyes, if indeed they have, and what did we see? When were we able to throw away one crutch, and then the other? Or do we still have them, stacked in the closet just in case?

We have not succeeded in answering all our problems—indeed we sometimes feel we have not completely answered any of them. The answers we have found have only served to raise a whole set of new questions. In some ways we feel that we are as confused as ever, but we think we are confused on a higher level and about more important things. So this report does not purport to give final answers, or to claim that we now "know how to do it." We see more need for revision than ever. But we *are* doing better than we did. And this is a progress report, rendered with humility because of the unsolved problems we see now which we could not see before.

We are fully aware of the fact that many people all over the land have contributed to the workshop idea. Currently many programs in many places are using similar techniques, and have contributed much to our thinking. Indeed, we could not have arrived at our present methods without their help. We are simply describing the program we know best.

CHAPTER II

Principles and Purposes

Over the years, certain principles, beliefs, and purposes have evolved. Perhaps not all of them came from the workshop itself. We started out with the over-all purpose of achieving a good educative experience for teachers so that they would teach better. We felt, and still feel, that the test of any educational experience in any professional school is whether or not the individual's attitudes and methods are better because of it. But this generalized purpose was not useful until we were able to sharpen and objectify it. This had to be done in the light of our beliefs and attitudes. Our beliefs come from what we are and what we see from day to day as we go about the business of trying one device after another. We have drawn upon what is now known about the nature of the human organism, and how it can learn.

The following set of guiding *principles* is what we can see to be true as of now.

1. *The most important thing about any person is his attitude toward other people*. We live in a social world, and life consists almost entirely of contacts and relationships with other people. The completely social nature of life has only recently begun to be understood. Our basic approach to others determines the kind of lives we live and the success we achieve. If we think other people have value, are ends in themselves, we will take certain approaches to them. If we hold other people to be only means to our ends, we act otherwise. The whole essence and meaning of democracy as opposed to authoritarianism lies here. The attitudes of teachers toward other people are perhaps even more important and crucial

4

than those of the ordinary citizen, as teachers are specifically engaged in the building of people. People is their stock in trade, their reason to be. Other people is precisely what the entire teaching profession is about.

2. *The primary need in the building of people is to learn better human relations.* This becomes crucial when we consider the social nature of life and the primary task of the individual in adjusting to other people. The business of communication between individuals and groups or nations is far more difficult than we have recognized. The evidence of failure in understanding each other is all about us. Misunderstanding leads to blameful attitudes, and eventually to the desire to destroy others. The building of people who can understand others and come to like them is so necessary that it seems doubtful whether we can survive without it.

3. *Every individual has worth, and has a contribution to make to the common good.* The schooling most of us came through does not cause us to feel that this is true, and too many of our teachers feel unworthy. They feel that nothing they could say would be worth listening to. This is obviously not the case. Every one of them is a bundle of accumulated experience, unique to themselves, impossible to find anywhere else. Every one of them knows some things, because of the unique nature of his background, that no one else knows. There is, therefore, much to be learned from even the least of us, provided situations can be set up where the dammed-up supply of experience can be released.

We see this more clearly in other walks of life than we do in school. In fact, when we allow people to think they have nothing to contribute, or even make them think so, we are denying the evidence all around us. If we were going on a picnic, or building a boat, or making a garden we would expect, without giving it a thought, that everyone would be able to contribute in some way. It is only in school that we seem to think that the leader, or a few of the "more able" are the only ones who can produce.

4. *Learning leads to more learning, and the human organ-*

ism is infinitely curious. Human beings are not lazy, except
in pursuit of the purposes of other people, purposes which
they have not accepted as their own. To appreciate the infinite
curiosity of the human organism one has only to observe a
young child going about his own business. There is nothing
which he does not want to investigate. This curiosity is often
dulled by his being required over a long period of time to
pursue others' purposes. The human being will seek knowledge
if left to his own purposes, and the building of new knowings
into his own experiences will lead him on to other activities.
Because he is more competent with each addition of experience, he will upgrade himself, since not to do so would lead
to repetition and boredom.

Thus it is that learning begets more learning, and each new
learning leaves unanswered questions. There is no rest in the
learning process, because each achievement presents new vistas
full of new problems. This is the essence of the fact that life
itself is process, and will not become static under ordinary
concrete circumstances.

5. *The most crucial learning at any given time has to do
with the individual's current problems.* This furnishes the
logical point of attack in any situation. The world is full of
things to be learned, but some are of more immediate concern to one particular individual than are others. The unsolved problems of the teacher's life and work become the
point of attack. The solution of these problems, if this ever
could be completely done, will lead to others more remote,
and, at least theoretically, will spread out indefinitely.

6. *Cooperation as a technique and as a way of life is superior
to competition.* When people cooperate, they are learning
about each other, depending upon each other, and developing
confidence in each other. The process throws people into
situations where it is possible for better human relations to
emerge. It is an attack upon the barriers that separate people
and tend to make them suspicious of each other.

When they compete, they must work alone, because to share

ideas or materials would help the competitor. This would hardly make sense. By working alone, to one's own advantage and to the detriment of others, the walls of isolation between people are built higher and stronger. These walls work directly against the improvement of human relations so essential to living in our complex society.

In the light of these principles, we have evolved the following *purposes*.

When it is possible for us to figure out what we believe in, we then are in a position to think about what we want to do. All honest and thoughtful action springs from beliefs held. We say honest and thoughtful action because not everybody follows his convictions. Some keep a weather eye on policy or on what others will think, and there is a disparity between what they seem to believe and what they do. Others accept automatic procedures, somewhat like rituals, established by habit and custom. These procedures are apparently unrelated to beliefs or to the nature of the organism to be educated. These procedures are thoughtless and do not necessarily reflect beliefs.

Accepting the foregoing principles and desiring to act upon them, it is possible to decide some things that we want to do. We call these *purposes*, and they must conform with principles held. We have evolved over the years the following set of purposes, or things we want to do.

1. *We want to put teachers in situations that will break down the barriers between them so that they can more readily communicate.* Knowing more clearly now than ever before the difficulty of communication, and holding that every individual has a contribution to make if it can be made, this objective takes on great importance. The individual lives by himself and is isolated unless he is put in a situation that brings him out of isolation and into communication. Living in isolation increases one's isolation, and the wall that separates him from his fellows becomes stronger. We cannot

learn from each other until isolation is mitigated and communication improved.

2. *We want to give teachers an opportunity for personal growth through accepting and working toward a goal held in common with others.* Growth in isolation is difficult. When people learn to devise, accept, and strive for mutual goals, it takes place rapidly, sometimes in veritable floods. We are growing organisms by nature, from the cradle to the grave, but this growth needs to be continuously stimulated by the surrounding circumstances. An individual, like a plant, may stand still in the matter of growth for years when the surrounding media are adverse, but this is a thwarting of the natural tendency of the organism, and any organism while it still lives can begin to grow again when conditions become propitious.

The development of a climate where growth will take place is probably the primary function of teaching. This is recognition of the fact that people are not taught, but learn. The function of the teacher is to arrange situations such that the student will learn—will be self-taught. It is precisely the same as arranging the proper amounts of soil, fertilizer, water, light, and heat so that a plant will grow. The gardener creates the proper environment but does not do the growing. It can best be achieved by working with others toward a common goal.

3. *We want to give teachers an opportunity to work on the problems that are of direct, current concern to them.* This is where learning can best begin. These problems have the advantage of being of primary interest to the learner, and of being nearby and easily arrived at. Further, current problems are the most practical and functional ones for anyone to be concerned about. A great impetus is given to learning when the learner can see that what he learns is immediately going to make his own life better, or easier, or more fruitful; when he sees that tomorrow will be better for what he learns today.

We have been slow to see that the logical place to begin anything is with that which is nearest at hand and of most concern. We have expended untold energy in trying to get people to do things that did not seem important or pertinent to them. We call it motivation, and volumes have been written on it. Motivation as applied in the classroom usually means getting someone to do something he would not do if he followed his own needs and purposes. When the learner works on his own current problems, expanding outward as new questions arise, he is motivated.

4. *We want to place teachers in a position of responsibility for their own learning.* In the traditional pattern of assignments and examinations, the teacher assumes the responsibility, while the learner follows instructions. In fact, the learner may even secretly defy the teacher to make him learn. Many of the teachers in our workshop have never before taken a course where they had to make any decisions as to what to do. It is the essence of learning to have to make decisions and assume responsibility. Many of our workshop members are confused because they expect the staff to tell them what to do.

School is one of the few places in life where people do not ordinarily have to make up their minds as to what they will do, and bear the consequences of those decisions. That may be why our citizens seem to lack the capacity to be responsible. Assuming the responsibility for one's own acts would seem to be near the center of the educative process.

5. *We want to give teachers experience in a cooperative undertaking.* Cooperation, like anything else, is learned in action. Not to know how to work cooperatively dooms an individual to isolation. When we consider the interdependent nature of human society and the closeness with which people must live together, the ability to do things with others, to accept a common goal and strive for it with others, becomes paramount.

6. *We want teachers to learn methods and techniques which they can use in their own classrooms.* What constitutes a good

learning situation for teachers applies as well to children. As teachers are now trained, they are loaded down with a heavy baggage that is of very little use to them when they face children who need to learn in accordance with *their* purposes. The problem is that of putting a group of growing individuals into a setting where growth can take place. Unless we have a chance to learn a better way through experience, we are apt to teach as we were taught, unaware of the human dynamics present in the class. By experiencing methods which permit teachers to grow in keeping with their own needs and purposes, teachers may learn how to arrange like learnings in their own classes.

7. *We want teachers to have an opportunity, in collaboration with others, to produce materials that will be useful in their teaching.* New methods call for new materials. Many textbooks are found wanting when children begin to learn about those things that are nearest to them and of most concern to them. Classrooms need to be filled with materials that will help children achieve their present purposes. Time, thought, and the help of colleagues are needed for the teacher to be able to furnish these materials. Of course the children will be able to do much about this problem, but they will need all the help they can get.

8. *We want teachers to be put in a situation where they will evaluate their own efforts.* This is closely related to the assumption of responsibility. When an individual assumes the responsibility for a course of action, he automatically judges how well his decision worked out. When he has made no decision, but has done what he was told to do, he lets the teacher do the evaluating, and cares little about it except as his grade may affect his future. The kind of evaluation that matters in the long run is what the learner thinks of his own performance. What someone else thinks is of passing moment, but what the learner himself thinks is built into experience and becomes literally a part of himself. This subjective evaluation furnishes guideposts for future action. It enables one to

correct false procedures, to revise decisions, and to attain goals. Goals can never be achieved unless people are put in a position where they can see how they are doing, and can make changes in direction and procedure in the light of this evaluation.

9. *We want to give the teachers an opportunity to improve their own morale.* Much of present teaching has been routinized to the point of boredom. This is especially true when the student is never given an opportunity to help in the planning; when he does not feel that he is a factor in what is going on, but is merely expected to carry out the decisions of others. When work is routinized and ritualized, the creative aspects of teaching disappear and morale declines.

Many of the teachers who come to us are suffering from lowered morale. They have feelings of futility about their jobs. This is detrimental to their work and to the children. Experiences which lead them to feel that their jobs are not futile tend to dispel this feeling. This is especially true when they have an opportunity to meet with others who have similar problems. They feel less alone in their boredom and futility. This is bound to be reflected in the atmosphere of their classes, and to have a direct beneficial effect on the lives of their children.

These are the principles and purposes we have come to hold. They are generally held by all of us in the workshop staff, although we would not all express them in the same language. They are the result of a process of growth on our part, as we have come face to face with real teachers having real needs. It is perhaps easier to hold beliefs than it is to do something about them. In the chapters to follow we will describe techniques and practices that we have used and are using in the implementation of these beliefs. Some of the details described may seem trivial and obvious, but it took us many years, in some cases, to learn them. Perhaps what seems trivial and obvious is only so because it has already been learned.

CHAPTER III

Procedures—How to Get Started

How can experiences be worked out to satisfy all the purposes set forth in Chapter II? We want to operate as a whole, so that we will be one group, not several. We want each person to have an opportunity to make his contribution, to provide circumstances where he will be able to do so. We want to be mindful of morale, and get at the specific problems of each member. There are so many values sought that the machinery necessary to bring them about is difficult to devise.

We can see that we will need to meet part of the time as a whole. If we do not do this, the workshop will have no entity, its members will not become acquainted with each other or have any feeling for the over-all enterprise. We will need to meet in small groups, because it is not easy for most of us to make contributions in large groups, nor is it possible to achieve specific goals with so many people involved.

We therefore meet (ordinarily, but not always) in a general session for a short time and in small groups for a longer time. Recently we have been meeting all together from 4:30 to 5:30, going to dinner from 5:30 to 6:30, and meeting in small groups from 6:30 to 9:00. We have found that the small groups need a good-sized allotment of time, while the large gathering is best if it is shortened. The primary purpose of the general session is to give the teachers a feeling of unity and solidarity and to lift their sagging morale, a condition that is apt to exist at the close of a day of teaching. Morale, however, is not lifted by too much listening.

12

The small groups need to be made up of those who have similar interests and who want to work on similar problems. It is rarely possible for a person to work on precisely his own narrow and specific problem unless he works by himself. But it is possible to find others who are interested in problems related to one's own, and when people with related interests get together, they have the situation which makes possible the choosing and acceptance of a group goal.

In the next few pages an attempt will be made to describe how we open the workshop in its first session and how we get the members into small groups of their own choosing, ready to work on problems in accordance with their own felt needs and purposes.

It is a Thursday afternoon late in September. Teachers who have enrolled for the workshop begin to arrive at about 4:15. They are a tired lot, for they have been teaching all day. They arrived at their schools at 8:00 or 8:30 in the morning. They have met their children, sometimes in great numbers and rapid relays. They have done their hall duty and lunch-room duty. They have been working with all sorts of children, from the kindergarten through the twelfth grade. Many of them have traveled an hour to get here. Some of them are past middle age, and have returned to teaching after having raised their families, and are hoping to bring themselves up to date in their profession.

There is only one marked difference among them. Some of them have been in the workshop one or more semesters and are greeting each other familiarly, calling each other by their first names, exchanging experiences of the summer, and recalling mutual experiences of the semester before. The others sit quietly by, not quite sure what such behavior on the part of the others can mean. These newcomers have an air of quiet apprehension, for this is a new "course" and they are not quite sure they will be able to meet the requirements and "pass."

In the front of the room is a coffee urn, with cookies, and the old members are quick to move up and partake. The others come up too, more reluctantly, and soon all are having coffee, although not all are participating socially. Some may take their coffee and sit down by themselves.

This informal social period lasts from about 4:15 to 4:45, since some of the students will not arrive until 4:30. People settle into their seats by that time, considerably relaxed. Then we have a few songs—the old favorites that everybody knows, although many of our new students will not join in the singing, but will look uneasily about and wish we would get on with the lecture.

The first song session is not entirely a happy one, but we can not have our second session until we have had our first one. The last singing session of each semester is high in participation. It would be interesting to record by sound and pictures the first and last such attempts.

After a few songs, one of the staff members extends a word of welcome to the students. He then attempts to explain some of the objectives of the workshop, and what the methods of procedure will be. He tries to give the members as much a feeling of security as possible. He does not talk over twenty minutes.

This speech does little good. It serves the purpose of getting the semester under way, and may give some members a feeling of confidence in the staff. We think the speech has to be given as a bridge to a different method of teaching, and if we made no attempt to explain what we were going to do, many would believe that if we had done so, then they would have known. As a matter of fact, attentive as they are, they do not really hear what we say because they do not have the experience with which to hear it.

Sometimes we have tried the following experiment. We have made the opening speech, doing our best to explain the process through which the group is about to pass. Then the group goes through the semester's experience, with all its frustrations and false starts. At the closing session we get out the notes that were used in the opening session, and give the same speech, word for word, as nearly as it is possible to duplicate without reading script. Invariably several members of the group will ask us why we did not tell them this in the first place, and save them all the frustration they have gone through. It is a neat demonstration of the perceptive value of experience—of the fact that a background of experience is essential to perception. It also demonstrates the weaknesses of precept per se as an educative device.

Following the opening remarks, if there is time, we ask the members of the group to write brief autobiographies. These help the staff to understand the individual members, and can be referred to as the semester passes whenever there is occasion to do so. These autobiographies sometimes tell us more by what they conceal than by what they reveal.

Early in the workshop we gather material for the workshop directory. The students fill out cards with routine data as to home address and phone number, school, grade, subject, etc. On the back of the card they list some of their major interests and areas in which they have had experiences that might be helpful to the others. This material is compiled and mimeographed and each member is given a copy of the directory. It is useful, because members who are working on certain projects find it helpful to be able to get in touch with other members during the intervals between meetings. Sometimes members are surprised to find that other members are near neighbors.

Before the first general session is over, the members are broken up into what we call problem-finding groups, so that they can meet in these groups after dinner. This process will be explained directly. The autobiography and the gathering of the directory data can be postponed if the time runs short. They should be done, however, as early in the semester as possible.

We are next confronted with the task of finding out what the members of the workshop want to work on, and how people with similar interests may be brought together. Early workshops required that people state their problems before being admitted. Implicit in this requirement was the idea that if the problem stated by a prospective member seemed trivial to the director, the applicant would be rejected. Indeed, we carry the impression that people *were* rejected on this basis. This seems contrary to what we know about what motivates people.

In the first place, there can be no such thing as a trivial problem, provided it is what is disturbing the learner at that particular time. Regardless of what others may think of the problem, that is precisely the place to start. Further, the necessity of producing a problem which will pass muster causes people to strain at the task, and often results in their coming up with something that is not their *real* problem at all, but something that will look good on paper. This is the best way to get a trivial problem. People do not always know at what precise point they should start on their dilemma. They may be in such a state of confusion as to be unable, at the moment, to identify their most urgent problems. Their lives and jobs may resemble a ball of yarn, with no good place to start to unravel it.

This can only be solved by reflection, cogitation, and conference with others of like confusion. As people talk together of the complexities which face them, they can help each other to see their problems more clearly. A great feeling of relief and camaraderie comes from the knowledge that the other fellow is no better off than we are. When we find that what he says applies to us, new understanding and empathy result.

So we have learned not to ask people to state their problems before they come nor, indeed, when they get there. Neither is it wise to accept the first point that is raised, for this may be the clutching at a straw, when a problem is expected. It is also apt to be true that, unconsciously, the student may deliberately substitute a "good-looking" problem as a front so that he can keep his real problems to himself. A superficial problem will usually bring out superficial work and solutions that do not matter.

In order to do as good a job as possible of getting at the real concerns of the individuals in the group, we put them into random groups for the purpose of talking the matter through. It is a good idea to have a staff member for each group, since the class members will not be too well accustomed to the small group procedure. If there are too few staff members for the number of students, making the groups too large, more groups than staff members may be formed, letting some staff members alternate between two groups and depending on students with workshop experience to assume leadership.

The problem-finding groups do best if they are made up of not less than ten or more than fifteen members. It will not do any harm to let the groups run less than ten, but they ought not to exceed fifteen. If there are ninety students and seven staff members, for example, it will work out well to have seven groups of about thirteen each. Many variations of this pattern will present themselves.

We like to form the groups by counting off. If we decide on seven groups, we count off up to seven and then start over. Thus all who are number one form the first group, and so on. The advantage of counting off lies in the fact that this method separates close friends who sit together and allows them to come into contact with people whom they do not know, but will need to know. This is a great advantage. If people who know each other well form a group, they are apt to say the same things to each other that they have been saying for years. To encounter new personalities and new points of view, and to share dilemmas with different people often throws a fresh light on one's whole set of circumstances.

It will be necessary to announce, not once, but several times, that these are temporary groups, not the groups people will work in all semester. Many teachers are fearful that they are being put where they do not want to be, and some of them will be so sure of this that they will not hear the first announcement of the temporary nature of the problem-finding groups. In fact, some of the close friends who have come together to bolster each other's courage will disregard the numbering and go together into the same group. If the staff member notices this, as he is apt to since this makes some groups too large and some too small, he had best say nothing at all about it, nor let it be known that he has observed it. It merely means that these people need each other for support and are not ready to be separated. The staff member can only hope that later on the socializing influences of the workshop will wean these people from each other to the point where they will not need each other's solace and support.

The problem-finding group, then, consists of from ten to fifteen people and a staff member. In the Wayne workshop there will be, ordinarily, a few in each group who were in the workshop the previous semester, but they may not know each other well unless they worked in the same interest group. There will be all ages and all types. The staff member suggests that they introduce themselves, giving not only their names, but such other information about themselves as they feel free to tell. It will not be necessary to choose a chairman because this is a free talking session, and it is temporary. The group will need a recorder, however, to record the ideas which persons in the group want to submit to the whole workshop. The staff member can see to it that the group's thinking is brought back to the purpose of the meeting from time to time.

The recorder is chosen informally. Since this is a man's world, the job is usually pushed off on one of the women, the one who has the pencil and paper ready. It is not a long-standing appointment, and is usually willingly assumed by someone.

It is likely that the first item of interest to the problem-finding group is the workshop itself. The members have just heard a short talk on it, and are curious about what is going to happen. This is a good way for these groups to get started, with the help of the staff member and experienced students. It follows naturally from the general session, and is apt to be uppermost in the minds of all. They may need to clear up in their minds what kind of a deal they have gotten into, preliminary to a consideration of what they are going to work on.

Now the group is ready to start talking about the problems that are close to them, and on which they would like to work. Some person may be surcharged, and come out with a whole list of items—a sort of catharsis of problems. The others will then join in. It may be, however, that all are reticent, in which case the staff member has to lead them into a discussion without setting the subject or tone of it. The group should be made to feel comfortable and relaxed; talk should be encouraged, even if it seems pointless or irrelevant. The people in the group should have an opportunity to just talk things through, it being pretty certain that ideas will crystallize out of this exchange.

The problem-finding groups should be allowed and even urged to stay in session as long as possible. If they can be held together for two sessions, so much the better. This is time well spent, because the more fundamental the problem the more significant will be the work of the whole semester. If the group settles on the first idea which comes to mind, interest during the semester may evaporate. If too much effort is expended by the staff member to hold the group, however, they will become bored with it. It is the function of the staff member in these groups to secure as deep probing as possible into the genuine concerns of the members, and to recognize the time when the law of diminishing returns sets in.

The recorder is supplied with 3 x 5 cards. Each problem should be put on a separate card. This mechanical device simplifies the classifying of problems after all have been turned in. It is important that the group pay careful attention to the wording of each problem.

The reason for this care can be seen if we examine the

reason for stating a problem at all. Suppose you are a member of the workshop, and are eager to work on one thing which is of great concern to you. You cannot very well work on it alone, so you hope that there will be others who will want to join you. It amounts to the fact that you hope your particular problem can be sold or will appeal to others, so that a group will form around it.

There are ways of stating a problem so that no one else will see anything in it at all. Others will not see that there is any place to grab hold of it, and it will not have the quality of putting people to work. The same problem, stated another way, may have the quality of releasing people's energies, and may suggest ways of leading people on to explore further. We see this quality in other types of teaching. Some proposals fall dead—put people to sleep. The same idea expressed another way may stimulate and energize a whole class. Therefore, the statement of a problem so that others will see ways to lay hold of it becomes important if you want others to work with you.

To illustrate this, the topic "School-Community Relationships" might not mean anything at all to a teacher, even though her most acute problem might be misunderstanding on the part of the parents of her children with regard to what she is trying to accomplish. She can respond to the problem "How Can We Get Better Understanding Between Teachers and Parents?" because she sees something specific in it for herself, and can perhaps imagine a way to go to work on it. To be sure, this specific is a small segment of the broader topic, but others will suggest other specifics.

When the problem-finding groups have completed their work, whether they use one session or two, the problems which have emerged are handed in to a staff member, one problem to a card. During the week which intervenes, one or more staff members has the task of classifying them into similar groups of problems. Many of them will be similar, and it is usually possible to classify them into about a dozen categories. For example, one category may be "Democratic Classroom Procedures." This may have from eight to twelve problems, all of which fall under this general title. Some problems may be so unique that they defy classification, and they are included under separate titles of their own. No problem is left out.

The problems in classified form are then mimeographed. Under each main title, the problems are reproduced exactly as they were stated on the cards. The mimeographed sheet, then, carries every problem in the words of the authors, but grouped according to subject—or given separately when this was not possible.

The following list of problems shows what came out of the problem-finding process in the workshop of the spring semester of 1950. It is in the form which resulted after staff members had taken the separate problems on the 3 x 5 cards and organized them under general headings. The main headings are generalizations made up by the persons who organized them. The subheadings are the exact words which the students put on the cards. There is no significance to the order. This depended upon what cards were picked up first, except that the single ones at the end were held out on the chance that similar topics might appear.

This list has no validity for any use anywhere except for the particular people who made it at the time they made it. It is neither a "good" list nor a "bad" one. It is what one hundred teachers in southeastern Michigan were concerned about in February, 1950. It is given here in the hope that it will enable the reader better to visualize what may happen when the problem-finding process is carried out. Many of the problems are not stated in ways designed to attract fellow workers, but it must be remembered that this list was made during the first and second meetings.

We have noted with interest during the years that the problems change with the times. During World War II we always had problems on the employment of adolescents, how to help children whose parents both worked, the children who were bereaved by the loss of father or brother, mentally and emotionally exhausted children, and so on. A glance at the following list will reveal that these problems have diminished or disappeared, while others have come into prominence.

Problems Proposed, February, 1950

1. *Techniques of Guidance*
   Group guidance
   Teacher-pupil relationships
   Contributions of mental hygiene to emotional and mental maturity
   How find out enough about the child's background to guide him?
   How use information and records?
   Understanding adolescent behavior
   Implications of modern psychology
2. *Adjustment in Early School Years*
   Children in kindergarten
   Transition from kindergarten to first grade
3. *Teaching Contemporary Affairs*
   Controversial issues (methods, problems, and techniques)
4. *School, Home, and Community*
   Understanding pupil problems originating in the home
   Home life in relation to child growth
   Relations between school, teacher, child, and parent
   Role of the teacher in the community
   Better school-community relations
5. *Critical Thinking and Social Responsibility*
   Developing awareness of need
   Propaganda analysis
   Evaluation of critical thinking
   Analyzing and interpreting situations
   Improving communication
   Areas of responsibility
6. *Human Relations*
   Integrating our culture
   Establishing interpersonal relationships

7. *Classroom Discipline*
   Classroom management
   Beginning teacher's approach
   Special education—speech, behavior
8. *Evaluation and Promotion*
   Continuous progress—teacher and group
   Testing
   Citizenship grading
   School dropouts
   The slow learner
9. *Teacher-Pupil Planning*
   Applying democracy in classroom
   Maintaining individual dignity
   Responsibility, individual and group
   Group work in elementary school
   Core curriculum
   Group dynamics
   Limitations and problems
10. *Staff Relationships*
    Cooperative curriculum planning
    Making teaching an effective profession
    Professional code for teachers
    Mental health of teachers
    Factors affecting group loyalty among teachers
    Study of preparation, growth, and development of school
       personnel
    Rules, regulations
    Teachers' meetings
    Getting teachers interested in professional problems
    Teacher-teacher relationships
    Problems of beginning teacher
    Problems of student teacher
11. *World Peace*
    The teacher's stake in UNESCO

When the workshop reassembles, we are ready to proceed
with the formation of the interest groups. These are the
groups which it is hoped will be permanent. They are formed
around common interests or goals. They are different from

the problem-finding groups, which were formed at random and had no common problem.

The mimeographed organized list of problems is given to the members, assembled in the large group. Each person is able to see his own problem, in his own words. Considerable time is devoted to seeing to it that everyone is satisfied with the way his own problem has been classified. Sometimes a member will ask to have his problem put under a different heading because it seems to him that it fits better there. These wishes are always respected. When everyone is agreed that the classification, as amended, is satisfactory, there is an opportunity for members to add problems which they may have thought of during the week. If there are any such problems, they are added, under the classification suggested by the persons submitting them. After this process has been finished, the list of problems as amended has the unanimous approval of the whole group. If it is not unanimous, we change it until it is.

Now we are ready to establish the interest groups. We ask each member to choose the one general topic on which he prefers to work. It is well to state here that these groups are not necessarily final for the whole semester. If a member gets into a group which is obviously not going to meet his needs, he can change. It also needs to be made clear that what the group actually works on will be set by the group, and may not necessarily correspond too closely to the original topic. Each individual will have a chance to help determine the actual goals of his group. This needs to be explained before the voting on topics begins, since some people will hesitate to make choices if they think they cannot get out of them. If each member votes once and not twice, the numbers recorded for each topic should approximate the number of members.

We may have as many as fifteen or twenty topics when the choosing begins. Some topics will poll large numbers, since teachers' problems are often similar. Other topics may not get any votes at all. This may seem odd since we might expect the person who proposed a topic to vote for it. He may, however, have been more attracted to someone else's proposal, especially since he has had a week to think it over. This free change must be encouraged and regarded as a healthy sign. Some people cling to an idea simply because it is their own. This pride in possession of an idea stands in the way of the release of one's own purposes. Many arguments and quarrels in life are caused merely by the fact that the antagonists have taken a position and have been possessive of that position *because* they have taken it. So when members freely abandon their ideas and adopt the other fellow's, it is a good sign.

If a single topic is chosen by as many as a third or a half of the membership, there need be no concern, because it is possible to split them into small groups, working on the same problem. One semester there were about thirty people out of ninety who chose "Democracy in the Classroom." They divided eventually into three groups of about ten each and worked well all semester. Although all three groups were formed under the same topic, they did different things.

The division of a large group should not be done arbitrarily, because it is usually possible to find a functional basis for division. The members should meet as a group of thirty and talk about the best method of dividing. Some will want to take up a certain phase of the problem, and others are apt to join them.

Occasionally a group of twenty or so will not want to divide. This is perhaps to be regretted, because we know from experience that this is too large a number to permit everyone to enjoy full participation. It is best, however, not to force a division. A forced division cannot be functional. After they have been together for a while and have explored the complexity of their general problem, they often divide because they see that their present arrangement will not work. Nature has another way of reducing the size of groups. If they stay together, some will see that their needs are not being met, and will join other groups. The large group may thus become medium sized in the natural course of events.

Some of the topics will have no votes; some will have one, two, or three. Usually those who are alone will make a second choice. Combinations are suggested which reduce the number of topics and increase the size of groups. No group should be less than three, and none should be so small if it can be avoided without violating the fundamental interest and rights of the members. Coercion at this point must be avoided, and the members themselves must be allowed to find a better way. Coercion would not be justified, even if the members went the whole semester without finding a better way.

Sometimes teachers from a particular school will come to the workshop with a definite notion of what they want to do. An example of this might be a group from one high school wanting to set up a guidance program for their own school. They are of course permitted to form their own group. We may ask them to help us with the problem-finding process, but they need not if they do not want to. We do ask them to take part in the general sessions, for this helps to make them a part of the total workshop.

It may happen that there is a person who can find no place in the scheme of problems where he can work with good will —with a heartily accepted goal. If there are a number of such persons, they should have an opportunity to meet together with a staff member to discuss their dilemmas. In this group situation they can tell what they had in mind, and, with the help of each other and the staff member, they may find places within the framework which they had not seen before. It may be necessary to set up some new situations which will more nearly meet their needs. Individual counseling should be available to all who want it in helping to find suitable goals. These suitable goals must be goals which will release energy in self-satisfying ways.

It may be interesting to show what groups evolved from the list given on page 22 from the workshop of February, 1950.

Only seven of the fifteen topics survived, because not enough students chose the others to make working groups. This made nine groups, because two of them, Teacher-Pupil Planning and Staff Relationships, were so large that they divided.

1. Techniques of Guidance
2. Human Relations
3. Adjustment in Early School Years
4. School, Home, and Community
5. Critical Thinking and Social Responsibility
6. Teacher-Pupil Planning—A
   (Elementary)
7. Teacher-Pupil Planning—B
   (Secondary)
8. Staff Relationships—A
9. Staff Relationships—B

Now we have our members divided into interest groups, and ready to go to work. This whole problem-finding process will have consumed two or three weekly meetings. They will meet next time on the new basis, and start the adventure of trying to clarify a common goal acceptable to all, and to work toward it.

CHAPTER IV

Procedures—The Interest Group

The total workshop is now divided into small groups based upon the interests of the participants. We will assume that if any group was too large for successful operation, it has already been divided by procedures suggested in the previous chapter. If the process of getting people into the right groups has been successful, which it never is completely, we are ready to proceed.

We do not mean to imply, however, that what has gone before was not work, or that the time consumed was wasted. The best time we ever spend is in finding what we are going to do and projecting methods of doing it. Time is never wasted when the human organism is contriving, for contriving is essential to growth. Most of the time that is wasted in education is wasted when the individual proceeds on the dictum of someone else to do something that is devoid of meaning to him. By doing this, it is possible to get into so-called "production" sooner, and to turn out more volume of "product," but we mistake the shadows for the substance if we judge growth on the basis of volume of material produced.

We are therefore not concerned with the length of time it has taken us to get into our interest or working groups. The participants have been in learning situations from the beginning. We can never do more than that for our students.

THE GROUP

A good interest group is made up of eight to twelve people. They are assembled because they want to work on the same general problem, although the specifics of what they are going to do remain to be established. The general problem has been evolved from them. This is of the utmost importance even if the staff had known from the beginning what the general area would be. Everyone in the group is there of his own free will. The course is elective, and no student is required to take it. The group he joins is up to him. He would be allowed to work alone if he insisted. The situation is so arranged that the specific group goal is worked out by those who hope to achieve it. There will be opportunity for each individual to make his unique contribution to the good of the whole, and to assume responsibility for it. There will be opportunity for planning, so that whatever each individual does will make sense to him. There will be chance for leadership to emerge, not only in the one or two people who assume the chairmanship, which is a superficial evidence of leadership, but among the whole group. For each will be leader when he has a unique contribution to make, and each will be follower when he learns from another.

THE CHAIRMAN.   Ordinarily the group will choose a chairman and a recorder. It is not always necessary to have a chairman, and groups have been known to succeed well without one. The smaller the group and the better its members know each other, the less likely are they to need a chairman. If the group is large, the members known to each other little, and the problem amorphous, then the choice of a chairman is essential.

Some groups have operated successfully by having a different person act as chairman each session. This has the advantage of giving the opportunity for leadership to everyone in the group at one time or another. It has some disadvantage in that no one person assumes responsibility for continuity and organization. Some people are more skilled as chairmen than others.

But we do not always get the most skilled person selected, and there is something to the idea that the unskilled need the experience more than the skilled.

The group, then, may have no chairman, a revolving arrangement, or a permanent chairman. The test is whether the group is going well in that it has been able to establish its group goal, is working successfully toward it, and has good morale. The chances are that if a group is not succeeding well, it should attempt to get its best-qualified member to assume the permanent chairmanship.

Let us assume that the group has chosen a chairman who, barring unforeseen events, will hold the post for the remainder of the semester. What ought he to do, and what are some of the errors he may fall into?

He is the one who holds things together. He should be extra-regular in attendance, and be there on time. If the chairman is ready to start when the time comes, the other members will more likely be punctual. If the members arrive on time and the chairman wastes from fifteen minutes to half an hour of their time by not being there or not knowing how to start, the members will also begin to come late.

The chairman must know what plans were made at the last meeting for the present one, and where to start to get the group going. He has given the matter some thought between meetings, and is prepared to make some sort of contribution by way of getting started if the group is "cold" and needs orientation to its plan. Much can happen in a week, and while members may have been excited about an enterprise when it was planned a week ago, they may have been through so much since that they need time and orientation to recapture their previous interest and enthusiasm.

The chairman does what he can to move action forward toward the objective which has been agreed upon. This he can do to a degree by bringing the discussion back to the central point from time to time when it seems to him that it has strayed into irrelevance. Holding the group to the task they have assigned themselves will be one of his most important and difficult tasks.

There are many reasons why this is difficult. The members of the group are usually unskilled in cooperative enterprise. They do not know how to work in small groups, because they have had so little opportunity to learn how. Yet this type of experience is important to them, for of all things they might learn in school, the one thing they are most certain to need is the ability to work with others, particularly in small groups. And this is especially true with teachers. In any decently operated schools, teachers are sure to be called upon to work with other teachers on their common problems.

There are two types of people, primarily, who make the life of a chairman unhappy. They are those who talk all the time, and those who talk not at all; and of the two, the former is the more harmful to the progress of the group. The worst group member is the one who has an answer to every question, and who is irrepressible. It is easier for the chairman to bring out and encourage the quiet one than to tone down the eager one. It does something to the morale of the group when the members know that whatever they bring up, the answer will be automatic, immediate, and final—and always from the same source.

It is not easy to say what the chairman should do about such people. It is obvious that exclusion would not be a solution because the eager one needs this experience more than the others. The chairman can direct an inquiry to another member, so that the eager one will not have a chance to kill the discussion before it starts. Or he can hope that the verbal catharsis will run its course, although this cannot be depended upon to happen before the end of the semester. Perhaps a staff member can counsel with the eager one. If the chairman attempts it, he should use indirect methods, as overt action on his part is likely to cause feelings detrimental to cooperative work.

We have said that the chairman should make an effort to

keep the group "on the beam"—to keep it rolling toward its chosen objective. This he should do within limits, but he needs also to have a wholesome attitude toward diversion, for not all diversion is bad. Sometimes, when the group assembles, there is something uppermost in the minds of its members which must be discussed before anything else can be done. He must not be like the teacher who refused to let the children talk about the invasion of Normandy while it was going on, but made them postpone it until the day for current events, even though some of the children had brothers taking part in the invasion.

A couple of years ago a local newspaper attacked the public school system and all its teachers. When the teachers met, their minds were full of this attack, and it was not sensible or even possible to expect them to go ahead with their self-assigned tasks without getting their feelings out of their systems. We can not expect them to stick to their work, even though it is self-assigned, when their minds need release and catharsis.

Diversion may be necessary at other times too. Sometimes the attack upon a problem may have to be roundabout, and what seems irrelevant may not be so at all. Problems do not always lend themselves to direct solution. It may take a good deal of "talking around" a problem before the method of solution becomes apparent. The chairman, therefore needs to be sensitive to the kinds of activity that will eventually yield progress, and not be impatient with the group as it goes about its work in its own way. He needs the skill to wait, and the skill to bring the group back when the diversion seems too remote or irrelevant. He must not consider time wasted as long as contriving is going on.

We must realize that when we insist that a group "stick to the point," the point we insist upon may not be the real point for the group. When ten people join together around a general problem, the problem is out of focus, although the questions under it are headed in the right direction. The point of attack is likely to be beside the problem, not directly on it. Often the original problem loses its significance, while new ones with real validity for the learner take its place.

A group in the fall of 1948 organized itself around problems of discipline. What the members wanted was to find out how to make children behave, what to do with the lazy pupil, and so on. Eventually they found themselves studying children, their growth, development, and motives.

An earlier group was organized to study methods of remedial reading. They actually studied methods of teaching reading so that remedial classes would not be necessary, and finally found themselves involved in the whole problem of communication.

The chairman must avoid the pitfall of talking too much himself. Some chairmen seem to feel that their function is to answer every question. This results in a two-way conversation between the chairman and one other member of the group. The chairman, when he accepts the post, accepts a specialized role of general overseer, and to a degree surrenders some of his rights as participator. He cannot observe what is going on when he is in the thick of it. This does not mean that he can never express an opinion, but he needs to be wary of it, because he can readily get himself involved so deeply that he cannot see what is going on. Perhaps a good rule to strive for would be never to say anything that he can get someone else to say. He usually has a chance to summarize the discussion, and here, by the very items he chooses for his summary, he has a chance to express his opinion.

The chairman needs to keep an eye on the morale, or the general tone, of his group. If morale is high, as evidenced by good attendance, eagerness to start, unmindfulness of the lateness of the hour, friendly atmosphere, the chairman has little to worry about. Conversely, when the group is reluctant to get going, attendance is poor, and the group wants to adjourn early, he may know that all is not well, and that the group is not doing anything which makes for the solidarity essential

to good group work, or which produces personal satisfaction
for the individual member.

The chairman should know when he needs help. Sometimes
this help can be found within the group. Often he will have to
look outside for it. He can call upon a staff member to help
point out the blocks which the group is up against, and to
suggest ways of getting over them. The chairman who lets
his group stay blocked all semester will finish with an un-
satisfactory experience for himself and all the others.

Any group needs a chairman who is sensitive to relevance
and irrelevance, who possesses enough tact to bring out the
best in each member of the group, who does not see himself
in the role of the teacher of the group, and who is willing to
sacrifice his desire to advance his own ideas in the interest
of general participation of the whole.

He will have an opportunity to practice leadership in its
best sense. He will have been chosen by his fellows, although
this in itself may not mean much. He will be in a position to
see that leadership in all its aspects emerges from the members of the group, and by tact and encouragement he can
bring it about that each member, even the most shy, has an
opportunity to lead. The wide distribution of leadership so
that each member feels he has led at some time is part of the
essence of good chairmanship.

THE RECORDER.   The recorder has an important although
less spectacular role. Whatever plans are made have to be kept
track of and brought into the minds of the members when they
start work. The recorder keeps the written materials, and
when the group decides to produce anything in writing, the
responsibility for getting it done is his. He may not actually
do the writing, and in fact it is better if he does not, but involves as many others as possible in it. But he is the one who
sees that it is done. If any communication to members between
meetings is needed, this is the duty of the recorder.

In the Wayne workshop, the recorder is asked to hand in
a blank to the staff at the end of each meeting. The blank

identifies the group, gives the names of those in attendance, a brief report of what went on, and tells whether or not the group needs help. This blank is of great value to the staff in keeping in touch with the groups. As long as the blank comes in, the group has an open avenue of communication and does not need to feel that there is no way of reaching the staff.

THE PROBLEM-SOLVING PROCESS

When two officers (or servants) of the group have been chosen, it is ready to begin work on its problem. Some time can well be spent in getting acquainted, although this cannot be achieved merely by formal techniques at the opening session. Each person can introduce himself and tell something of his work and his special interests. This helps a little, but the members of the group will not really know each other until they have worked and played together.

The operation of the group is no different from that of an individual in a normal problem-solving situation except that there are several people involved who need to be consulted instead of one.

A true learning situation is a problem-solving situation. It is common in life outside of school on an individual basis. The individual starts with wanting to do something. He has a goal which is his own and therefore worthy, in his opinion. He figures out how he wants to go about it. Then he proceeds to try to do it the way he decided would be most likely to succeed. If he seems not to be achieving his goal, he stops and asks himself whether or not there was anything wrong with his plan. He revises his plan and tries again. This time he may succeed, or he may have to change his plans again. If he cares enough about his goal, he will continue to contrive until he reaches it. It is simply a matter of having a goal held to be worthy, making a plan which seems likely to achieve the goal, trying the plan, evaluating the failure, re-planning, trying it again, revised in the light of experience and achievement. This is what we all do all of the time, and it is the essence of the learning situation.

The only place in life where we do not follow the typical learning procedure, oddly enough, is in school, where people are presumably assembled for the express purpose of learning. This defection is complete, from the first grade to the doctor's degree. In school the goal is furnished by the teacher, and may or may not be worthy to the learner. Whether the learner holds it to be worthy or not is a matter of little or no concern to the teacher. The plan of attack is given by the teacher, and the teacher watches to see that the plan is carried out as directed. There is no need for evaluation along the way because the plan is sure to work, since it has worked many times before. Achievement is automatic as long as the tested plan is followed, but satisfaction of achievement is lacking because the goal was not one which the learner really cared about in the beginning. He has been denied the adventure of contriving. The learner has come in for the least interesting part of the process, and there is little in it for him except work. He has missed the exhilaration of holding a worthy goal and achieving it.

Successful group work would be easy if it were not for the fact that other people are involved; in other words, it would be easy if it were not group work. Arriving at a common goal and releasing the energies of several people in a concerted attack on the problem is the difficulty. It is also the point of greatest reward, because each individual enriches all of the others, and the profit to each member of the group is far greater than in solitary action. But the steps are the same, and are simple. If they are kept in mind, the complexity of joint action will be the only complexity involved.

THE GOAL.   No group can accomplish anything until it has figured out what it wants to do. This seems elementary, but many a group has failed because it never clarified its goal. This, then, becomes the first order of business. The group must stick to the clarification of its goal until everyone in the group knows what the group wants to do and accepts it as worthy.

Establishing a goal which all can accept is not easy. It may call for a good deal of compromise. There is the advantage that the people in the group are together because they have a common general interest. But what one individual sees in a general topic may be quite different from what another sees, and this needs to be carefully worked out. It may come about that one person is unable to accept the goals of the great majority. This person may need to withdraw from the group and join another, or get the counsel of a staff member as to where in the total workshop there may be a spot where his present felt needs are apt to be met.

The topic which has brought the group together is often too general to put people to work. It needs to be made specific, so that each member can see something that he can do about it. Energy is released on specifics, not on generalities. We usually have one or more groups meet together to work on the problem of democracy in the classroom. The popularity of this topic, which nearly always emerges from the total group and is never injected by the staff, shows that many teachers earnestly desire to learn how to get rid of the autocratic methods they have inherited, and teach more democratically so that their children will have some preparation for citizenship in a democracy. But the topic itself will never motivate anyone to action.

One group, met together around this topic, made it specific by listing some questions which gave the members places to take hold. Some of these questions follow. "How can I organize my class so that every member will have a chance to contribute? How can I find out what goals my learners can accept? When and how can I use small group techniques? How do I go about teacher-pupil planning? How can I work with my pupils democratically without having them get out of control? What kind of planning can young children do?" This list of questions made the general topic meaningful, and gave the members of the group ideas as to how they could begin. It sent them to books, to staff members, and to colleagues for information.

The specific goal of the group should be arrived at through consensus. This means that it is talked through and modified until every member of the group can accept it as worthy. No group can succeed if there is a minority which cannot accept what the group is going to do. Such minorities will exist if the chairman resorts to voting as a means of gaining a decision. Parliamentary practice—the motion, the second, the vote—can ruin any group that is planning to work together, because it divides the group instead of bringing it together. Full discussion, understanding, and compromise can achieve goals which all can accept and on which all can spend themselves. This is consensus.

Once the specific goal or goals have been agreed upon, they need to be put into writing, and copies need to be supplied each member. These written goals should be constantly in front of the group and regularly referred to; all planning should be done with these goals clearly in mind.

THE PLAN. Having agreed upon what the group is to do, the next step is to plan how it is going to do it. This will probably involve a long-time plan and a short-time plan. The group can lay down ways of going about the whole thing so that the semester will end with achievement. This is essential, but it does not tell each individual what he can do about it tomorrow.

The short-time plan has to do with what the group is going to do next Thursday evening, and what each member can do between meetings so that he can be a more useful member of his group. Without this short-time plan, the members will come back in a week just the way they went out, so far as the group project is concerned. They will have missed the opportunity to increase their value to their fellows.

What members do between meetings so that the goals will be brought nearer will take on many forms. The first thing many of us think of is reading. And indeed it may be that the member may profit by looking up some literature on the topic to be considered. This is only one way of preparing to be a good member the next week, however, and may not be the most fruitful way. Some other and more promising experiences are that he may try something in his class, or he may talk to others whose experience and judgment offer something, or he may consult his students who are the consumers. He may profit most of all, on occasion, by thinking about the problem himself, and coming to some tentative conclusions in that way. When he feels that he has made progress in that way, he will gain respect for his own thinking. Many of us have been trained not to respect our own thinking but to feel that we have to depend on the thinking of others. This leads us to acceptance on authority, whether what the authority says makes sense or not. We are particularly inclined to accept if the "authority" has succeeded in getting his ideas printed. We have undue reverence for the printed page, not realizing that the author is usually just another person like ourselves who has accumulated material and had it printed.

The long-time plan needs to be put in writing. The short-time plan need not be. The last few minutes of every session should be devoted to what the group is going to do at the next meeting, and what individual members can do to make the next meeting successful. Of course if the group already knows what it is going to do, then this short planning session is not needed, but in most instances it will be.

THE TRY. Now we put into operation the plans we have made. Here contriving which bears directly on the goal begins. This will probably extend over a number of meetings.

THE CHECK-UP. All members of the group, and particularly the chairman, must watch the try, to see whether the goal is likely to be reached by what is going on.

It is not altogether a matter of approaching the goal, although that is important. There are other factors and conditions to be watched. Is there general participation? Has every member been involved? Is the morale of the group good? Are the members becoming better acquainted and coming to enjoy each other's company more? Is the attendance of the group good? Do they work their full time at each meeting, or do they usually adjourn early? Do members of the group begin to find that there are errands they have to do which cannot be done any time except when the group meets? Are they at a loss as to what to do when the meeting starts?

Some of these symptoms may reveal the fact that the plan is not working. The members of the group had at one time expressed interest in what was projected, and if that interest has evaporated, it seems likely that the plan needs to be reconsidered.

THE PLAN REVISED. When symptoms indicate that all is not well, a session is needed to discuss the reasons. This discussion should be as frank and free as possible. To the degree that it can be done, every member's ideas should be brought out. If poor attendance is a problem, it might be helpful if the recorder would notify each member by mail that a gripe session has been scheduled. Disaffected members are more likely to show up for a gripe session than a work session, especially if the work sessions have been unrewarding.

In this session, the weaknesses of the plan as it has operated can be brought out, and revision can be made so that the members will feel that it will now work. It may be necessary to discard the old plan and substitute a new one. The defects of some of the personalities may come out in such a way that they can be accepted, and these persons may learn from this how to become better group members. Some may have driven others away by their talkativeness, others may have failed to do anything to make the group succeed.

This check-up meeting ought to have the help of a staff member unless the presence of the staff member reduces freedom and frankness. This should not be the case if the staff has succeeded in establishing the proper relationships with the workshop members. If the members of the group feel that a particular staff member is the cause of the breakdown, then the group will do better by itself or with another member of the staff. The chairman should be in the best position to decide whether a staff member should attend and who it should be.

Try Again.   Further contriving is now in order, in the light of what has been learned and through the use of the revised plan.

THE ACHIEVEMENT

There is no way to tell how many times the plan of action may need to be revised. As in life, we can never be sure that any projected action will take us where we want to go. No plan can ever be said to be a good plan until it is put to the test through concrete action and has brought the results which the plan was intended to bring.

In the contriving, which is the putting of a projected plan into action—with the struggle and frustration which is usually entailed—the greatest amount of learning occurs. In order for real learning to come about, the group must have freedom to plan wrongly, and to learn through action that they have planned wrongly. More is to be learned by making mistakes in planning and execution than in perfect performance.

Of course this can be carried too far. If a group makes so many mistakes in planning and execution that it never gets anywhere, never makes any progress, feelings of futility will eventually dissipate the energies of the members and the group will disintegrate. This will not ordinarily happen. If a group pursues a fruitless path for a time, this experience should show it a better path, not a worse one. But there is nothing to be gained by artificially forcing better planning. There is more learning to be gleaned from finding out that the group cannot do what it projected than there would be in having an outsider do its planning for it.

In most cases, when the end of the semester comes, the goal will have been achieved, and the satisfaction which comes from ultimate success after much contriving will be felt. The significance of the goal will lose some of its importance, because the process will assume greater importance. The possession of the achieved goal will bring satisfaction, to be sure, but no specific set of materials or ideas can become as important, once achieved, as the contriving which brought the goal into being. The skill acquired in working with other people will abide with the individual members of the group long after the materials constituting the goal become outgrown and insignificant. This skill is the one thing we can be sure will be needed by all human beings in a social world, and this is especially true of teachers.

One of the human values to come out of successful group operation is that the members will continuously grow in their respect for each other. They will continuously get to know each other better, and to find value in each other. Out of their contriving and frustration there will grow a group solidarity, with everyone belonging. The members will discover, often to their surprise, that these are really remarkably fine people they have been thrown with. A sort of "one for all, all for one" blood brotherhood comes, which often means much to people who by habit and training have been solitary workers, and who have felt growth stunted through the loneliness of the human spirit.

As to the specifics of the achieved goal, doubtless there is more satisfaction felt if the members of the group can carry away something tangible and in writing. This will vary with the type of goal which the group has established. Some kinds of goals probably cannot be achieved without writing. An example of this might be the production of a source unit on China to be used with later elementary children. The goal itself implies and demands a written document, and cannot be reached in any other way. Another goal, such as a better understanding of motives behind common human behavior, might be achieved by mutual verbal contributions, and not necessarily call for any writing at all.

This brings up the interesting question as to how much writing a student ought to do at any time. We are all accustomed to the term paper technique, and to other requirements for writing. The usual term paper is unrelated to the goals held by the student, and, indeed, often unrelated to the goal of the teacher, except that the teacher holds a vague goal that he wants the student to work hard, and that a certain amount of travail is the price of credit. These requirements go on year after year in spite of the obvious sterility of the performance. The student accumulates many pages, often by copying them out of books or from other students' previous papers. The teacher, in many cases, does not and cannot read them. He cannot read them because they come in all at once at the end of the term, and they are so insufferably dull that the teacher cannot keep awake while trying to do his duty. So he "hefts" them, turns the pages to make sure that no blank pages have been "hefted," and grades them on the basis of the apparent labor involved.

The only possible purpose for writing is communication, or the accumulation of usable materials. The doing of the writing demands that the writer become specific, and the specifics have to be agreed upon by the group through consensus. If the writing is done for communication, then it must consist of what the writer wants to communicate, and it must be read by the person or persons for whom the communication is intended.

The answer, then, to the question as to how much the members of a group should write is that they should write as much as they need to in order to accomplish what they set out to do. There is apt to be added satisfaction if the members of the group have something tangible and material to carry away with them, particularly if each feels that he helped produce it. There should be no writing done purely to satisfy someone else that work has been done, and that they have paid the price for credit.

Criticisms of the group process are frequently heard. They

come from people who have been members of groups which have failed to achieve their goals and have therefore failed to bring satisfaction to the participants, and from those who have never tried to be members of groups. They sometimes come from people who drop in on a group once, and, being unable to see where the group started or where it is going, go away without any notion of what has been going on. It is doubtful that such people are really motivated by an honest desire to see what is going on, since they would never want their own work to be judged by such a brief spot sample without orientation.

Many of the criticisms are true in specific cases. We cannot guarantee a successful experience to anyone, any more than he can guarantee it to himself when he attempts something outside of school. Some groups never do get anywhere. The main consolation is that all teachers must work on a percentage basis, and there is no teacher anywhere who has no students who did not profit.

The critics say that there is a great deal of confusion in the group process. This is true. There is confusion wherever real learning, with genuine contriving, goes on. This is true even when people are working by themselves, and it is multiplied when it involves a number of people. The only time there is no confusion is when one person establishes the goal for all, and enforces the action toward it. Democratic procedures require the involvement and consultation of many people, and this results in confusion, or what may appear to be confusion to the superficial observer. The more people involved, the more contriving, the more confusion, and the more learning. In education, beware the machine which runs too smoothly!

Sometimes we hear that group work is nothing more than a bull session, where everybody has his say and nothing eventuates. Some groups do this, and while there is some profit in such sessions, they are likely to play themselves out, and become less and less fruitful. The difference between good group work and a bull session is that in group work the group has an agreed-upon goal, a plan, and is working toward the goal as best it can. A bull session has no goal and no plan.

Some feel that if thrown upon their own, students, even mature teachers, will not work. No one will ever do anything unless someone makes him do it. This is a very commonly held belief among teachers at all levels, and often a teacher who is a student at the university believes this of his own students while resenting it when it is applied to him as a student. The democratic faith calls for a belief in the general rightness and goodness of people, and one who lacks faith in other people lacks the first requisite for democratic teaching. It is true that a person will balk, or be lazy, when forced to pursue the purposes of another. But it makes no sense to assume that he will not spend his energy in the pursuit of his own purposes. The trick to getting people to spend their energies, then, is in finding ways by which purposes acceptable to them can be arrived at. When we hear a teacher proclaiming that other people are lazy while he is not, we are puzzled to know where and how he came into possession of such virtue, while others were denied it. The only tenable position on this matter for anyone to take, it seems, is that no one has a corner on virtue, that people will move when they see something which to them seems worth moving on, and that if they are lazy and perverse, it is best to look to see what goals fail to move them.

Some say that when a group works together all they get is pooled ignorance, and that nothing times nothing is still nothing. There is more than one fallacy revealed by such a statement. In the first place, the members of the group are not ignorant. Each has a lifetime of unique experience back of him, and each has a unique contribution to make. People have been adversely conditioned for so long that the student himself may be persuaded that he is of no value. It may therefore take time and patience to bring him out so that his experiential background can become useful to his fellows. The person who believes in democracy must believe in the unique worth of every individual and must seek ways of making that worth come out, and only an autocrat could possibly say that a whole group of people have nothing to contribute.

In the second place, the contributions of the members of the group may seem trivial to an outsider, particularly if he holds himself to be superior. But no problem is trivial if it is of concern to the individual at the time. This is precisely the place to start, and it is indeed the only place where a start can be made. As growth takes place, and as the self-confidence of the members grows, the nature of the problems under consideration will also grow, and they will become more and more significant when judged in relation to the total educational scene.

This discussion of the groups has been an oversimplification, but is written in the hope that it will be of help to struggling groups. If group members will watch just two things, a great part of their trouble and the danger of failure will be obviated. The first is to have a specific goal stated in writing for the semester, to which they frequently refer and in the light of which they do their planning. The second is never to adjourn a meeting without knowing what they are going to do at the next meeting, and what each individual can do between meetings so that he will come back prepared to do his part for its success.

A well-known principle of mental hygiene is that the individual must have a worthy task, a plan, and freedom. This was expounded twenty-five years ago by Burnham,[1] and probably many times before by others. This is what the group must have, and the enthusiasm of group members who have come through a successful group experience is due, we believe, to that fact.

[1] Burnham, William H., *The Normal Mind*, New York City: D. Appleton & Co., 1924.

CHAPTER V

Procedures—Resources

No interest group needs to "go it alone," without help from the outside. A group's greatest resource is its own members, and to the degree that they are able to work out their own problems by themselves, to that degree are they likely to derive satisfaction from the total experience. We have the greatest respect for the so-called "addition of ignorance," for what each has to offer will determine the proper starting point for such learning as can be experienced by any one group at that particular time. Enrichment of this experience can be had from sources outside the group, provided we never lose sight of the fact that it is the experience agreed upon by and derived from the group that is being enriched and expedited.

THE STAFF

The most important and most readily available outside resource is the staff. During the entire history of the Wayne University Education Workshop we have had a staff of from four to ten people whose chief reason-to-be has been to help the groups operate more successfully. We now have six staff members, three of whom have served during the entire ten years. Three of the members are full-time faculty members of the College of Education. One is Admissions Officer at Wayne University. The others are former workshoppers, employed on a part-time basis for this assignment.

We have never quite solved the problem of knowing how to use the staff. We are not certain that there is any completely satisfactory answer. We have tried many ways, and we have yet to operate a workshop where we felt that each group had the proper help at the proper time. This is partly due to the difficulties involved in the geographical location of the groups as they hold their meetings. Often they are badly scattered, since rooms are always hard to get at Wayne. But for the most part the difficulty lies in the fact that being a useful staff member, helping the group to grow in its own independence, and keeping the final responsibility for progress squarely on the members of the group is a skill which is very difficult to learn. There is not one member of the staff who would claim to have mastered it, although we know more about it and do better at it than we formerly did.

Most of us are inclined to say too much. We are teachers at heart, and we are too apt to feel that we have the answers. It is easy for us to take over a group meeting entirely, giving too freely of our dubious wisdom. The group, too often, is too willing for us to take over. The members have a long history of listening, assuming the passive role. It is perhaps more or less natural for them to throw responsibility to someone else, and we teachers, unless we watch ourselves, are likely to grab it.

We have tried many devices. At one time we formed as many groups as we had staff members, and assigned a staff member to each group. This hardly makes any sense at all in retrospect, because if the problems are derived from the felt needs of the students, we have no way of knowing how many groups we will have. The groups came to bear the names of the staff members, rather than being known by what they were organized to do.

One difficulty with this method of using the staff was that there was a tendency for the staff member to become the teacher of the group, and this resulted in our having a number of little classes, much as if there had been no workshop at all. The second difficulty with the method lay in the fact that students tended to join the group which had the staff member they wanted to hear. Since some staff members had greater reputations than others, and since some really were more interesting than others, the groups became uneven in size. Occasionally a staff member who was less known would find himself without any students at all. There was a tendency to develop a listening situation, with lack of student responsibility. This came about through no intent of any member of the staff, but was the natural outcome of a faulty method, and perhaps a lack of skill on the part of the staff members in knowing how to throw responsibility on the students.

In an effort to improve this situation, we then decided that no staff member would be attached to any group, and that no staff member would ever stay with one group long enough so that the group would begin to feel that the staff member belonged to that group. We even went so far, at one time, in our effort to throw responsibility on the groups as to agree that no staff member would visit any one group for two consecutive meetings. We agreed to visit groups on a random basis, and not to stay too long.

This did not work either. Some groups went too long without any help from the staff at all. Others got too much, or if not too much help, too much interference. Sometimes three or four staff members would be in a group at the same time. If the group had a goal and a plan, this excess baggage made it hard to operate. Sometimes the staff members even engaged in a discussion among themselves, which was quite paralyzing to group process.

It happened occasionally that a staff member would tell a group something and leave, to be followed by another who would tell it something contradictory. This can happen where people of good will operate in a free climate, even when the two people are in accord on most things.

Perhaps the basic difficulty with this method was that no staff member stayed long enough in any group to be able to see what the group was trying to do. Without some knowledge of what is being attempted there is really nothing a staff member can do except to give out his own miscellaneous ideas. Staff members, like anyone else, have to be put in positions where it is possible to be helpful before they can do anything constructive.

The problem, then, is to set up a situation where the staff member can be helpful, while the responsibility lies directly and firmly upon the members of the group, and where the staff member will be only a resource as the group contrives to find its way to its goal.

The system of distributing and using the staff that we have employed most recently is a compromise between the two methods just described. During the time that the groups are getting started there is no designated relationship between groups and staff members. While the problem-finding groups are meeting, each staff member meets with a designated group. But after the interest groups are formed, the staff is generally helpful but actually does little. In a week or so, after we are sure what groups we have, we hold a staff meeting and give each staff member about two groups for which to be generally responsible. This provides for some overlapping, but that is held to be desirable. The staff member is expected to know the members of such groups, and to know what they are doing and how they are getting along. Since no one staff member is expected to know about every group, it is thought that he can be fully oriented to one, two, or at most three groups. By this method, no group should be neglected, and no group should have too many staff members visiting it at any one time.

Whenever questions arise with regard to any student, we know from the weekly report what group he belongs to, and we can generally get information concerning him from the staff member who has assumed responsibility for that group.

It is not expected that a staff member will never be seen in any other group than those assigned to him. He may attend any group he wants to, and there may be times when it is best for him not to attend the group he is responsible for. Or he may visit any group on invitation. If the group is studying something concerning which a staff member is known to be well informed, the group can invite him as a resource person.

No announcement is made to the students concerning this division of responsibility. This prevents the switching of groups by individual students in order to be with certain staff members. Of course the students eventually figure it out, since they see certain staff members often and others seldom. But by this time they have become oriented and interested in their groups, and usually they are unwilling to leave for superficial reasons.

We think this arrangement works better than any other that we have tried. It keeps the responsibility on the students, makes sure that no group is neglected, and prevents students changing groups to be with or away from certain staff members.

So far we have dealt only with the problem of getting the staff member into the right group at the right time. This problem has bothered us over the years, but it is simple compared to that of deciding what a staff member should do after he gets in the group. This is a situation calling for great tact, and none of us has completely mastered it. There are many delicate nuances to which one must be sensitive if he is to maintain an atmosphere where each individual will do his best. The staff member is a status person, whether he wishes to be or not, and one wrong word or gesture, one harmful attitude, can set a group back for weeks.

The members of our staff do not want to be status persons. We would like to be just people, working with other people. But of course there are differences inherent in the situation. We are more experienced than most students, having been around longer. Some of us have titles and degrees which stick in the minds of our students, causing them to defer to us. Students see us in the role of persons of power so far as grades and credits are concerned. Then there is the indisputable fact that we are being paid, while they are paying. So we have trouble convincing our students that we want to be human among humans.

The barrier in our culture between teacher and student is difficult to overcome. It probably goes back to the European teacher, from whom our teaching was copied. It is developed over many years by wrong and autocratic teaching methods. It is promoted by insecure teachers who are posing as authorities when they know their limitations but do not intend that students should find them out. Students in the democratic teacher's classes find it difficult to believe that they will not be put upon before the time is over. If he tells them he will not trap them, they do not believe him. They say it may all seem fine in the beginning, but there is a catch somewhere. What abominable human relations we teachers must have practiced for generations to deserve such attitudes!

The staff member needs to do everything he can to build confidence with his group, so that the students will accept him at his human value. This takes patience, and one little error will set the staff member back immeasurably.

Assuming that we have the right staff member in the right group at the right time, and that he has been able to establish satisfactory rapport between himself and the group members, he then has two distinct and different roles to play. He will do better if he keeps these in mind, does not try to mix them, and knows which role he is playing at any given moment.

The first is that of *expeditor of the group process.* The group is to have its own goal and its own plan and, after these have been established, the activity should be that of making progress toward the goal according to plan. Groups often break down. They come to a spot where they seem to be stuck, and cannot themselves see how to get beyond this point. They do not know how to "get over the hump." The staff member should be able to diagnose the trouble and make suggestions as to how they can get on to what they have set for themselves. Whenever a staff member enters a group he should orient himself as quickly as possible to what the group has been doing and is now attempting. Then he can judge as to whether the group is rolling along or milling around. Often some simple suggestion will start them moving. If the suggestion is in the form of a question instead of an answer, it is usually more likely to be effective. A staff member can render a group the most service as expeditor of the group process.

The other role is that of *resource person*, where the staff member has knowledge and experience that bears on the problem the group is trying to solve. Often, however, the staff member may not know more about the problem than the students, because the problem was not chosen with him in mind, but was derived from the needs of the group.

The staff member should be more familiar with the literature of education generally than the students. He should give all of the assistance possible, because there is no sense in making students hunt for material that is readily available from the staff. Life is complicated enough without doing anything the hard way. But the staff member must be careful that he gives help at the right time. The time to do this is when the group, in following its plan toward its goal, comes to the point where this information is needed. Information should never be gratuitously offered in a general way, but should be offered when the unfolding of the plan calls for it.

We all have had experiences where we were invited to serve as resource persons in a group when the group was not ready for it. To illustrate, I was asked to come into a group to "talk" about student participation in school government. When I attempted to orient myself to what the group was doing I discovered that it had never established a goal and had no plan. The students had heard that I had had some experience with student government, and had thought that it would be nice to listen to me hold forth about it. I made an effort to redirect their efforts toward getting them to figure out what they wanted to do, and, as tactfully as I could, threw the responsibility back to them. I told them finally that when they had figured out what they wanted to do, and when added knowledge of this problem was called for, I would be glad to help them, not only with my own experience but also with such knowledge as I had of the literature. This is not easy to do, because one runs the risk of offending the members of the group, thus introducing an emotional element which blocks action. It needs to be done, if possible, because if it is not done the staff member becomes little more than an entertainer or time-filler.

The staff member will do well to keep his two roles in mind, to know which one he is filling, and to realize that his chief value lies in the role of the expeditor as the group tries to find its way toward its goal. The role of resource person based on wider knowledge will only occasionally be appropriate. The staff is the groups' most important outside resource, because it should be able to keep the groups moving toward their own goals. No other outside resource is in a position to do this.

READING

Probably the second most important resource as the group contrives to reach its goal is that of reading material. It lends itself especially well to the needs of the group because it can be taken home and used between meetings. This saves the time of the group and this is important since the amount of time available to the group for its meetings is limited. It is also valuable because it provides something a group member can do between meetings to make himself a more worthy member of his group. It is one way by which a member can come back to the group a better member than he was when he left the last meeting. The feeling of satisfaction one derives from knowing that he has made some effort to facilitate the progress of the group is of great value to his general well-being and his feeling of adequacy.

Nothing said here is intended to depreciate the value of the written word, or the help that students can secure from it. The printed page is one of the great methods of communication. It has one handicap, however, and that is the fact that it is one-way communication, and best results are obtained where it is possible for two or more human beings to communicate back and forth. The best communication is no doubt the twoway, give-and-take kind. The printed page, however, makes it possible for one to communicate at least to a degree with other humans whom he will never be able to see. It makes possible the accumulation of the history of the race and its culture. Through the printed page it is possible for those long dead to give thoughts to the present inhabitants of the globe.

One of the tragedies of educational method is the misuse of reading. This misuse causes damage to the student's attitude toward reading, so that he may become unable to use it for what it is good for. The printed page and its reading have become ends rather than means. Some of us have even come to believe that the harder the reading is the more value it has.

The errors of teachers in the use of reading as an educative device are many and grievous. The first of these is the habit of assigning specific required reading. Aside from the fact that not all members of a group of people need the same reading, nor can profit from it, the greatest damage is done to the attitude of the student toward the material read, and to reading in general. If I take up a book because I have been coerced and therefore have fears regarding it, my whole tone and attitude is different from what it would be if I picked it up because I wanted to know what it contained. With this adverse attitude, I am on the look-out for items which the teacher may ask me about. It is a boring performance, and the pages may begin to stick together, and turn several at a time.

The requirement of a certain number of pages of reading for a course is unsound. If a student is required to read five thousand pages for a course, he will, if he has any sense, pick out the books with large print and wide margins. If the book has some pictures, so much the better. He will never be able to afford to read periodicals, because often the pages are large, and the print small. We may wonder if the education of our "educated" people does not usually consist of such ideas as are printed in large type with wide margins.

The customary book reports also damage the reader. It is true that they are often required as a means of getting the student to organize the ideas of a book (which we trust have already been organized by the author). Too often book reports are required as proof that the student is not lying when he says he has read the book. Thus it sometimes comes about that an air of suspicion is established between the teacher and the student. This causes the student to do things which he would not formerly have considered. Because of the climate of distrust, he may even write a fine book report without having read the book at all.

Unfortunately, one of the differences between life and school is that in life one is innocent until he is proved guilty, and in school he is often held to be guilty until proved innocent. Our most rigid, autocratic, and conservative teachers thus are guilty of un-American activities.

This discussion of the bad uses of the printed word is presented because the staffs of many so-called workshops fall into this error. Perhaps they do this because they do not believe that other people have the same virtue they attribute to themselves, and they are not ready to use the motivating power of present need to move forward. It is apropos here because we have ourselves had to learn this the hard way. We were in the beginning all cluttered up with meaningless reading requirements and futile reports. When this particular scale fell from our eyes, the quantity as well as the quality of reading rose.

There is only one good reason why any human being should open a book, and that is to find out for his own use what is in the book. If he reads a book for any other reason, he will learn little and his attitude toward the printed page will be damaged.

There are, in the main, two basic kinds of reading. One is

for pleasure or for general enlightenment or enjoyment. This is valuable, and will be more extensive if people are so educated that they have a good attitude toward reading. The other is reading for information which will serve in the solution of a current problem. This is the kind which will be most often used by students in a workshop, because they are struggling with some current problem.

The amount of reading will depend upon the amount of material available and the time of the student, as well as his speed of reading. Some students will read rapidly and have considerable time for it. Others will have less time, depending on their jobs and other responsibilities; and they may be slow readers. So the volume read will vary greatly among students. This will be expected, and perhaps even cherished, if we believe in the fact and the desirability of individual differences. When one reads for help in the solution of a problem, he is not likely to read whole books, but will often read the parts which bear upon the problem he is trying to solve. He will not persist in reading a book which has no meaning for him, but will take another which seems more profitable.

Availability has a great deal to do with the amount that workshop students will read. These are in-service teachers. They come to the campus once a week for the most part, and during that time they are kept rather busy. It is all very well to tell them that there are rich resources in the college library, or in the city library, but the truth is that they will usually have neither the time nor the energy to use these resources.

To meet this need we operate the workshop library. This is a collection of about a thousand volumes, placed on open shelves in a location convenient to the students. We buy about fifty volumes of new publications each year and dispose of some of the less-used books, so that the collection remains about the same size and is fairly up to date. The books cover well all of the curent problems in education, and material can be found here which bears upon most of the problems the groups may encounter.

We do not maintain a librarian. Students are urged to spend time looking the collection over. When a student sees a book he would like to take home, he writes his name and the date on the card and leaves it on the desk. He is asked not to keep the book longer than he needs it, but is permitted to keep it as long as he wants. An effort is made to get the books back at the close of each semester.

We lose a few books through accident and neglect. But we do not lose as many as we would if we hired someone to watch the students, and to look through their brief cases as they come and go, as do some libraries. There is no way to prevent people who have developed bad attitudes from stealing books if they put their minds to it. The best safeguard is in building relationships which will make people want not to steal from us. While we lose from five to ten volumes a semester, we believe that we have never lost a book through deliberate intention. Often the missing book will be one we do not care much about anyway; if it is one for which there has been considerable demand, we reorder it.

The use given our library is astounding. The vitality and newness of the material, the easy availability, and the eagerness of the students to help themselves and each other—all are shown in the stretches of vacant shelves. None of this reading is done under compulsion, and the reader is responsible only to himself for what he gets out of it.

Reading and the workshop library, then, are probably the most important outside resources, after staff. We think we have eliminated most of the abuses which have grown up in education with regard to the value and uses of the printed word. Our students read what they want and need, but reading is always a means, never an end. Our students often continue reading after the course is over. The usual required reading assignment is terminal in its nature, in that when the requirements have been met, the student has no desire to read further in that area. A good educative experience should be so planned that it is only the beginning, and will be largely continued long after the course is over. Stated another way, any course which ends in its interest and activity at the close of the semester is most likely to be a failure. The reason for saying this at this point is that one of the easiest and most likely ways of putting continued interest into action is through reading; and it is because of the abuses of reading that so many courses close with the final session.

OUTSIDE PERSONS

A resource often used is that of a person who is not attached to the workshop but is invited in for a specific reason. This may be any person in the whole community who happens to know something about the particular problem at hand. In Detroit our resources in this regard are great, although we probably do not utilize them enough. If the group is working on a good program of guidance, it can invite a principal or a counsellor from a school having such a program to tell how he does it, and what the blocks or difficulties are. If the group is working on the improvement of school-community relations, a superintendent who has a good program may be helpful. This is an extension of staff as resource person.

The outside resource person can give information, and perhaps inspiration, but he cannot facilitate the group process. He should not be invited until the group has determined its goals and its plan of action and has come to the point where it needs outside information.

When a group is not going well, usually because it has not defined its goal and plan, and the question arises as to what it will do next week, someone is most likely to say "Let's have a speaker." Another will say "I heard Mr. So-and-So last week and he gave a wonderful talk, and I'm sure he'd be glad to come."

This is an escape from the real business in hand, a shift of responsibility from the group members to someone else. The chances are if this person is invited he will talk engagingly, and all of the members will enjoy it. Some will positively purr because all they have to do is listen. So habituated are we to listening—to the lecture method—that we become most comfortable when we can again relinquish responsibility. The contribution of the outside person may be excellent; in fact it usually is, because the person is known for his ability before he is asked, and, since he probably will not be back, he can "shoot the works." The trouble with it is that if the group does not have a goal and a plan, the contribution of the outside person cannot fit the goal or plan. If it does not fit, it becomes miscellaneous and will thus have a fleeting effect.

This does not imply that outside persons cannot be useful. They can be useful, and we ought to use them more. But they must not be used to shift responsibility, or for entertainment. They are most valuable when they are invited at a time when the information they have to offer will bring the group nearer its goal.

VISUAL AND AUDITORY AIDS

The same can be said for visual and auditory aids. Extensive resources in such things as movies and filmstrips have recently been developed. They often are more effective than the outside speaker, because they present perceptions for both eye and ear. Through them, groups can be shown how something may be done, as well as being told about it. Also, a movie or filmstrip can be viewed without imposing on the time of an outside person.

These aids are subject, however, to the same criticism as the outside speaker. Any group planning to use them should make sure they fit in with what the group is trying to do. It too often happens that when anyone suggests that we see a movie, everyone thinks it a fine idea, without regard to the nature of the film. The relinquishment of responsibility can, of course, be even more complete when viewing a movie than when listening to a speaker. The room is dark, and usually warm. Thoughts can wander at will, and consciousness may depart without the fact being known even by one's own colleagues.

The repeated emphasis on responsibility is made here because it is the serious challenge in the operation of a workshop. There is no intention to imply bad faith on the part of the students. But to many of them it is the first time in their educational careers that they have been called upon to assume any responsibility. We all have a desire to return to the familiar, and an escape from a situation to which we are not accustomed is always welcomed. The staff sometimes yearns to return to the authoritarian methods they know so well, and are thus no more virtuous than the students. How to keep the responsibility where it belongs, and not weaken, is the most difficult problem of both staff and students.

FIELD TRIPS

It sometimes comes about that a group may find that it suits its purpose to go to some place in the community where something is going on, a knowledge of which may enhance group progress. A group that is working on intergroup relations, for example, might find value in visiting a synagogue, or a Catholic church service. It is regrettable that in our workshop it is not possible to visit schools to see programs in action because of lack of time. The group members seldom can do this on their own because they are in-service teachers, and are working when other schools are in session. Much could be learned by this type of observation if it were possible.

Sometimes a lecture which serves the purposes of the group is being given somewhere in the city. Certainly the group should feel free to attend it, without any feeling of neglecting duty. Most lectures will not serve the purpose of the whole workshop, although occasionally one does. Ordinarily, outside lectures should therefore be attended by small interest groups, if at all.

The operation of a large number of miscellaneous field trips has ruined many a workshop. The learnings are scattered, and not apropos. Part of the members go, and part stay, but those who stay are usually too few to do anything on the problem which the group is trying to solve. There is value in one's knowing his community, and it is valid to organize a learning experience centered around this. But it is best, then, not to attempt any group work. This would not be a workshop as we define it, because the heart of the workshop is the interest group, where a small number of people attack a problem of common interest.

It is hardly possible to introduce and describe all of the resources to which an interest group may turn. The use of children, and of children's work, such as art, creative writing, autobiography, etc., should be mentioned. The members of the group should be continuously on the alert for such items which should be used wherever they serve.

CHAPTER VI

Procedures—The General Sessions

Each time the workshop meets, part of the time is devoted to a general session. There are a few exceptions to this, but not many. This session is held at 4:30, which is the starting time. It usually lasts until the workshop goes to dinner. The dinner hour may be moved forward or back, to allow the amount of time needed for the general session. Thus the weekly workshop experience consists of a general session in the beginning, a dinner hour, and small group meetings.

The general session is necessary because it enables the whole workshop to do things together. Some reasons for this have already been discussed. If the workshop consisted entirely of small group meetings, the groups might actually do better than they do now, since lack of time is one of the problems which confronts them. But what seems to us of greater value is to have the total group held together. This is good for morale, and enables members not only to get acquainted with other members, but to realize that they are not the only ones who have problems. Without the general sessions, we would have eight or ten small groups in operation, with no relationship between them, and no total workshop would exist.

In spite of the importance we attach to the small group, where specific goals and plans are possible, we believe that there are some things that can best be done in the large group. If a lecture, for example, is worth while, it will almost always be a better lecture if the audience is fairly large. Group singing, a builder of morale on which we depend, is best with many participants. Information of common value to all can most efficiently be given if it is given only once. There are also certain announcements that are best made here.

We hold the general session at the beginning of each day's activities for a number of reasons. If the meeting is any good, it gets the members off to a good start—it picks them up. Announcements often apply to that day's activities, and therefore need to be known at the start. If the small groups met first, going to small group meetings directly from a hard day's work might be somewhat dismal and depressing. Being an effective member of a small group, with attendant responsibility, is the hardest school work there is, bar none. We do better when we rest them and feed them before we expect initiative. The "rest" of course is not exactly that, but it consists of planning programs, however serious, in which most of the in-service teachers can assume somewhat passive roles.

Being fully persuaded, on many counts, of the value of the general session, we are then confronted with the problem of what should go on in them. We have struggled with this down the years, and have produced no answer which completely satisfies everyone.

In the early days we solved this problem by operating what amounted to a Chatauqua. Each Thursday afternoon we had a speaker, usually someone not connected with the workshop and preferably someone from out of town. We watched for visitors who were passing through on other errands, and inveigled them into giving us speeches. We usually assigned no topics, letting the visitors speak on whatever was uppermost in their minds at the time. We seemed to operate on the theory that any speech is a good speech. We did not, of course, believe this, but what we were doing was the only solution we could think of at the time. The students enjoyed this and we would never have changed at their request. Many of the speakers were stimulating and entertaining, and the in-service teachers were all too willing to go along.

Always a little unhappy about the miscellaneous character of this educational experience, and often put to it to provide visiting experts, we finally came to the conclusion that, since the work of the small groups was the heart of the program, there was no sense to any general session that did not facilitate the small group process. We therefore banned all speeches or lectures which were given for the sake of a speech alone. This does not mean that we never have an outside speaker at the general sessions, but it does mean that we never have one who does not fit the over-all program of the workshop. We recently listened to a lecture by Ashley Montagu on the biological and scientific basis for cooperation. This is an example of the type of outside lecture that makes sense in the workshop. It enabled members of the small groups to see reasons for working together.

There are about sixteen general sessions to account for all together. The first meeting is taken up by general orientation. There are many things to explain and announcements to be made. The staff is introduced, and often we have had each staff member make a few remarks as to the meaning of the workshop to him. We start here to try to diminish the differentiation of staff and students to the end that eventually there will be little difference in the minds of anyone. We begin to try to achieve the informal relationship which we hope will become common before too long. There has to be some way of getting started, but it does not matter too much what is said here, because this type of educative experience is so new to the students that they will not hear much of what is said. It is a neat demonstration of the fact that no one can hear anything which is said unless he has some experiential background with regard to it.

At this meeting we lay the ground for the problem-finding groups described in Chapter III. The meeting serves the purpose of getting started, and forming these groups. If it is well done, it should leave the students stimulated and curious, and should release their anxiety and give their energies paths to follow.

The second and third meetings will be needed for carrying out the problem-finding purposes as described in Chapter III. The second meeting will be required for small group discussions where problems are brought out and stated. The third general session will be occupied with going over the mimeographed organization of the problems and making decisions as to which problem the individual wants to work on.

The next two or three meetings should be used by the staff to do what teaching it can do to help the interest groups in their work. The interest groups at this time are just starting in a tentative way, and usually they are fumbling in their attempts to get going. This is an opportunity for the staff to give them some help. If the members of the groups do not see the essentials of group progress (the long and short goals and the plan of action), they will not progress.

One session spent on the essentials of group work can be profitable. This can be followed by a session on problem-solving in general. There will be other ways and means open to the staff, depending upon needs which have developed, the kinds of people in that particular workshop, and the abilities and imaginations of the current staff members.

THE PLANNING COMMITTEE

A discussion of the student planning committee is introduced at this point because one of its major concerns is the planning of the general sessions. This responsibility for the general sessions should be moved as quickly as possible from the staff to the students. This is consistent with the general belief that the assumption of responsibility is educative and should rest whenever possible with those who are to be educated.

Some workshops are ready to assume this responsibility earlier than others. It depends upon the amount of experience present in this sort of activity, and to a minor degree it depends upon the progress of the groups. It cannot well happen before the fifth general session, but it should certainly be established by the seventh, so that the staff's responsibility ought to be over when the sixth session is over.

Our planning committee is chosen by having one member from each interest group, chosen by the group. This member meets with the committee and acts as contact person between the committee and the groups. The committee has to work out its own meeting time. This has been a serious problem with us, because our time is limited. It is not desirable for the committee to meet during the general sessions, and it is almost as bad for it to meet while the small groups are meeting. When the latter happens, each group is deprived of one of its more active members. We have tried having members chosen who could meet at 3:30, an hour before the general session. This has the advantage of making it possible to bring the decisions of the committee to the attention of the workshop at the start of each general session. It has the disadvantage of putting the planning into the hands of people chosen on a time basis rather than on a basis of planning ability, or of being the real choice of the group. Sometimes we cannot even find people who can come an hour early.

Recently the planning committee has been meeting during the dinner hour, eating together and extending their meetings as long after dinner as need be. This has obvious disadvantages, but it is perhaps as good an arrangement as we can have as long as we work with teachers who are carrying heavy loads in their jobs.

The planning committee has other matters to look after besides the programs for the general sessions, but this is probably its most important function. The committee does all the planning from the time it is formed until the workshop is over, except the planning that goes on in the small groups. The two most important matters in addition to the general sessions are the social events and the evaluation, both of which will be taken up later.

The committee will of course need a chairman and a recorder. In addition, it chooses the general chairman of the workshop. Sometimes the chairman of the planning committee is also chairman of the workshop. This general chairman has the over-all responsibility for the success of the whole semester. He takes charge of the general sessions, in place of a staff member, making announcements and introducing those who are to participate in the program. The planning committee need not choose one of its own members for this responsibility. It can choose any person in the whole membership who, in the opinion of the members of the planning committee, will be most capable of carrying out this task.

It is helpful if one member of the staff can meet regularly with the planning committee. This is a difficult and exacting assignment. The staff member has to be able to help the committee without becoming the end-determiner. He must be able to help when help is needed without robbing the committee of its freedom, its need for initiative, or its responsibility.

The reason help is needed is that the members of the committee are being asked to plan for something with which they have limited experience. They are only beginning to learn the workshop methods which they are expected to plan for. When we look back over the years and see how long it took the staff to learn facts which now seem simple and obvious, we can see what the position of the student planner must be.

If the committee and staff member will keep in mind one thing, they will be likely to meet with a degree of success, and often they will succeed triumphantly: Whatever goes on in the general session must facilitate or bear upon the small group process with which all of the workshoppers are struggling. This is the type of activity that binds the workshop together and gives it unity and purpose throughout.

The question should be "What can we do that will make the small groups go better?" When the committee does not stay on that beam, it too often becomes "What can we do to fill in the time?" The test of any program, in the planning stage, is whether it will have any bearing on what the members are trying to do.

Someone may want to know why it is that this committee needs help—cannot go it alone. Does this not apply to all other planning in school, and is it not all a sham, really under the control of teachers and staff members?

The planning committee is essential to the proper operation of the workshop because it gives the members a feeling of ownership and of responsibility. If we wanted a neat package we could of course plan it better ourselves. But we are not interested in a neat package. The package can be and often is too neat for realizing the educative process. Even if the program is a poor one, it still has the merit of being the students' program. If the program failure becomes revealed and analyzed through student evaluation, it can become a learning experience in spite of its mediocre success, or because of it.

The degree of help needed in all planning is relative to the stage at which the planner is and the intricacy of what is to be planned. Little children can and often do decide what they want to do and do it without any help. Outside of school we plan as individuals continuously, usually without help. This becomes more complicated and difficult when others are involved, and it becomes group planning. But there is never any sense in denying anybody any help that is available through others with more experience, provided that the one giving the help does not become the end-determiner; provided that it does not come about that the person who was supposed to furnish the help changes roles with the one to be helped, so that the teacher becomes the doer, and the student the helper.

The planner, at all levels and in all cases, should have the help he needs if it is available, up to the point of interfering with his own contriving. The younger he is, either in age or in specific experience with the task at hand, and the more complex the task, the more help he will need. The planning committee of the workshop, in planning programs for general sessions which will facilitate small group process, is up against a problem with which its members have had little experience. Even the staff, which has struggled with the problem for years, does not know how to do it to its own complete satisfaction. It is therefore only common sense to give the committee the benefit of such experience and wisdom as we have. The place to draw the line on help is where the staff member is taking over the planning.

In planning the general sessions the committee needs to beware of any program that commends itself because it is easy or entertaining. The temptation is always present. The members must ask themselves each time what this program does for the unity of the workshop and the facilitating of its major task.

There are many devices that can be used, and the committee should look first at the resources to be found among the members of the workshop itself. Occasionally the members of an interest group that is going well can tell, in an informal discussion, how they got going and what the whole perform-ance is meaning to them. Not only do other members get some good tips on what they may do, but they are likely to derive inspiration from a presentation by an enthusiastic, successful group.

The general sessions can be used to keep the members in-formed as to what is going on in all of the groups. One of the perennial complaints of students is that they know good things are going on which they are missing. To the degree that they can be informed, it is a good idea to do so. Of course no one can ever have the experience of a group member without being one, and without staying through the entire process. One student spent the whole semester running between groups because she knew there were good things going on which she was missing. The result was that, because she never became a continuing member of any group, what she saw in each group was fragmentary and lacked meaning to her because she was not oriented to it. If a person is having an experience in one place he cannot be having it in another, and good things are going on all over town, only one of which can be taken in at any one time. Some might feel that we should not have allowed her to paddle about thus, but after all, it was her educative experience, not ours. If we had required her to attach herself to one group and stay there, she would have fretted, and probably missed the experience anyway.

Programs can, however, be planned that will give the whole membership some idea of what is going on in all the groups. This is good to do to the extent that it can be done. It adds to total group unity. The planning committee can ask each small group if it wants to take over a program. Some will not want to particularly, if they feel unsuccessful, but some will; and these can be scheduled.

The staff need not be left out of these programs. The planning committee should feel free to call upon the staff members for anything it wants them to do, and the staff members should feel more or less obliged to do what they are asked to do. Sometimes the committee has asked the staff to constitute a panel for discussion of a particular workshop, as to how it is succeeding in comparison to others, and what the staff can see as indicated next steps.

Ordinarily it is a good idea to close the semester with an over-all evaluative session. This is in addition to such evaluation as individuals and small groups may want to do. The evaluative session can take any one of a number of forms, and therefore calls for careful planning. The planning committee may want the students to fill out forms which the committee devises, and this needs to be set up in time for it to be done. Specific techniques for the evaluative session are set forth in Chapter VIII.

In order that the reader may see clearly what goes on in the general sessions, the following recapitulation may be worth while. There are usually sixteen sessions in the semester, although the workshoppers often get so interested in what they are doing that they operate seventeen or eighteen sessions. On the basis of sixteen sessions, the first three are devoted to getting started, and getting the working groups established. The next three sessions will ordinarily be taken over by the staff. This is because the planning committee is not yet ready to assume them. In these three sessions the staff, in one way and another, tries to give the large group help on the fundamentals of group process. This may consist of lectures, discussions, demonstrations, or panels. They deal with ways by which a group may succeed, the learning process, and problem-solving.

About three of the remaining sessions are taken up with evaluation. These are usually the last three, although the planning committee may decide to have an evaluative session any time, and is likely to do so if the members feel that the workshop is not going well.

This leaves approximately seven sessions, which occur in the middle weeks of the semester. All of them are set up by the planning committee. All are designed to facilitate the group work.

These consist of the following types of meetings:

1. Progress reports by the small groups. Any group that wants to may take a session to show what it has been doing
2. Panel discussions by students
3. Panel discussions by staff or outside people, provided the request comes from the planning committee
4. Sociodramas, usually concerning the roles of various types in small group work, or to portray the progress of some particular group
5. Moving pictures, or filmstrips, which bear on the problem of group work
6. Lectures, if the planning committee can find someone whose lecture will bear on what the workshoppers are trying to do

Whatever use a workshop makes of these seven sessions, it has no validity for any other group at any other time. What they do is what they can contrive to do, under their particular circumstances. The above specifics will be useful only in permitting the reader to see what has on certain occasions been contrived.

The general session, then, is an important part of the workshop. It gives unity, and serves to lift sagging morale. It gives the staff an opportunity to teach such things as can be taught under such circumstances. It gives the students an opportunity to plan and to do something as a whole. It helps to break down, to a degree, some of the barriers that interfere with free communication between people.

CHAPTER VII

Procedures—Ways of Reducing Barriers Between Learners

Education is primarily a matter of communication. Discussions as to whether or not it should be experiential are really concerned with the question as to how best to communicate what is to be had in fact and attitude. Getting new knowings past the outer defenses of the individual and into his inner being so that they become functioning parts of him is the educator's primary business.

Language is our main tool for communication, but it is limited, and functions none too well under the best of circumstances. We all attach different meanings and feelings to words, and we can hear only the words, or concepts, for which we have some experiential background. To secure understanding it is often necessary to express an idea in a number of ways, and to have an opportunity for questioning. The inadequacy of words can be overcome to a large degree when there is opportunity for two-way communication—for give and take.

Language in the form of the printed page makes possible communication when the one giving the concepts is absent. This is of course a great asset, because it enables us to receive from those who have gone before, or who are removed by distance.

Teachers have long labored under the false impression that to have spoken is to have been heard, and that to have read is to know. This one-way communication, whether spoken or written, depends upon the receiver being both able and willing to receive the ideas expressed. We know that even when the hearer appears to be attentive his thoughts may be many miles away, and the words may have fallen on deaf ears. Lack of attention is not the only cause of deaf ears. Often when the hearer earnestly "puts his mind to it," he fails to comprehend what has been said, either because the words used have different meaning and feeling content for him, or because he lacks the experience to understand. Teachers who rely upon lecturing and reading operate under this misconception, and fail to a degree to accomplish what they try to do. This misconception of the nature and difficulties of communication may cause such teachers to blame their students, when the difficulty lies with their own teaching method.

The problem of communication is further complicated by the fact that we all carry barriers around with us which must be pierced before new ideas can penetrate to the inner functioning self. These barriers are our natural defenses, and we keep them—build them higher and thicker—as long as we feel we need them. They are perhaps the greatest obstacle to communication, and their reduction and dissolution is the primary concern of one who would teach.

We would all have these defenses, to a degree, even if life as lived did not tend to build them up. They are inherent. Each has his own ego to enhance and defend. Each seeks ways by which he can strengthen his ego, but an obvious part of this enhancement is also its defense. We are not all that we would like to be, and consequently not all that we hope others will think we are. We therefore try to cover up our weaknesses by preventing others from seeing too deeply into our real personalities. The more deeply we feel our own inadequacies, the more we try to hide them by building an outer person which we show to the world, and which no one is permitted to get behind. The inner guarded person is forever lonely because no one can join him. The wall gives a certain sense of security, but it prevents the acquisition from the outside of those knowings, attitudes, and concepts which would enhance the individual. The defense, built up, then becomes the nemesis of enhancement. Social intercourse is reduced to a trickle, and since social relations are the essence of life, life itself, in its significant aspects, is reduced.

Unfortunately, many of the customs of our culture, and many of our educational practices, tend to build these barriers. Many hold the attitude that children should be seen and not heard, and that the child is too immature to have a worthwhile opinion. Carried into school, life there too often becomes a matter of listening and reading, but not one of giving out. This trains the child to have a low opinion of himself, and to have little respect for his own thinking. He becomes persuaded that what he has to say cannot be of any importance. The more he is persuaded of this, the more defensive of his inner person he becomes and the stronger he builds the barriers behind which he hopes his poor weak self can abide.

Many teachers think that the way to deal with an individual is to "cut him down to size." They do this by taking the first opportunity, when the student comes out of his shell and says something, to use sarcasm or ridicule to "put him in his place." These devices are used by small people who do not want anyone around who is bigger than they. So they "make him feel small." He retires within his shell, which seems roomier than it was before he "stuck his neck out."

So prevalent is this feeling among the students in our workshop that often discussions start by someone saying, "Well, I don't want to stick my neck out, but—" This has become the Great American slogan. It is the turtle state of mind. It is a characteristic acquired by the lives people lead, in home and in school. It is anathema to communication, and hence to education.

Communication before it can take that name, has to pierce these barriers. It is best when it is two-way, so that words can be used again and again toward the achievement of understanding.

Two-way communication is in keeping with the democratic ideal, which holds that each individual is worthy, and that each has a contribution to make to the good of the whole; that each knows something no one else in the group knows.

To educate, ways have to be found whereby back-and-forth communication can take place. This calls for techniques that tend to reduce barriers between people and to build confidence in each person in his ability to contribute—and confidence in others, in that they will receive his contributions in good faith and respect. It calls for the building of the inner self to the point where its owner will think it has competence, and therefore does not need so much defense. Respect for one's own opinions and one's own thinking has to come before a person can become a contributing member of a group.

We engage in a considerable amount of activity in the workshop that is designed to reduce the barriers between people, to coax them out of their shells, and to make them feel comfortable outside their shells. A great deal of this activity may look like "horseplay" to the casual observer. But we do not do it for fun, or because either the staff or the students necessarily enjoy it. Many of the students really suffer, especially during the opening weeks of workshop. Many feel that they are being asked to "act foolish" and are uncomfortable. To such students, this participation is much more difficult than any assigned book lesson could ever be. They would give anything to be able to take a book assignment off in a corner while the "nonsense" is going on. We do not indulge in these activities because we want to, but because the reduction of barriers between people is essential to two-way communication. The more one hates to participate, the more he needs to.

There are, without doubt, other ways by which people's barriers can be broken down—by which they can come to know and respect each other—but we do not know what they might be. If life is social, and if we are bent on increasing social intercourse so that people may work together, it would seem that the barrier-reducing activities will have to be social. Some of the activities we have used are described below.

We encourage the use of first names. This draws people together, perhaps superficially, but wherever it can be done consistently with the current standing of the people in each other's estimation, it helps. We say little about it, but we do it ourselves to the degree we can, and thus tacitly encourage others to do so.

To insist on this practice, as has been done in some workshops, is as artificial as to forbid it. One cannot comfortably call another by his first name until he has grown with that other in mutual confidence and respect. To force one to call another by his first name when he cannot do so comfortably is to create a tension which will defeat the purpose. As we work together and grow in mutual confidence, first names are heard more and more. This is a symptom of growth, and shows that people fear each other less—need less to defend themselves in this company.

There once was a custodian on a university campus whose name was Patrick O'Hara. He was an institution in himself, known and loved by all. He was known to all as Patrick.

A new president came to the university, bent on upgrading the standards of the place. In due time, he called Patrick into his office.

"I notice that everyone calls you Patrick," he said, "I am calling you Mr. O'Hara, and I am issuing an order that everyone else on campus do the same."

"Oh," said Patrick, "don't do that! They wouldn't know who you meant! I'd lose my whole personality! Why don't you want them to call me Patrick?" "Well," said the president, "I wouldn't want people calling me Egbert." "Oh, Dr. Himmel," said Patrick, "nobody would do that! You have to know a person very well and respect him very highly before you can call him by his first name!"

We often serve coffee at the beginning of the session. There is, perhaps, a physical justification for this practice, since the teachers arrive after a long day of teaching. Many of them have had to hurry to get here on time, and auto parking is a rather exhausting experience in our vicinity. The coffee gives a physical pick-up which is usually very welcome.

It does more for the teachers socially than it does physically. They sit around in groups visiting, often getting acquainted with new people. The whole process is relaxed and informal, contributing directly to the values we hold. The coffee period has another value, in that it is usually furnished by one of the working groups. This means that it is not only paid for by them, but is ordered, transported, and served by them. What is left has to be gathered together, used cups disposed of, and the containers returned. This is a physical service which the small group can do for the good of the whole. The whole process tends to make more possible those activities for which we are assembled.

We usually open the general session with singing. There is something about singing together that brings people closer to each other. It is an activity in which they can engage without being too conspicuous, as they are being coaxed out of their shells. Or, if they are too inhibited, they can refrain from the refrain.

In order that inhibited people may not be too relaxed during the singing, we make a good deal of use of action songs. After one has gone through the appropriate actions of "Do Your Ears Hang Low" or "Little Tom Tinker," it is difficult to return to the role of the stuffed shirt.

We have an opportunity to develop leadership through group singing. We usually find someone among the students who can lead the singing, or play the piano. In our repertoire of songs we have a number that have been contributed by students.

We eat dinner together. In spite of enormous difficulties, we have stuck to the point that one of the best ways to socialize a group is through eating together. It is as though the organism, when it opens its mouth to admit food, also opens its personality for intake of whatever socialization is available. This is of course well known and used everywhere. It is the reason for the service club, and for refreshments at the Parent-Teacher Association meeting.

In the early days we used to think we needed to plan some activity during the dinner hour. We learned, however, that the relaxed approach is the best, and that people like to relax, eat, and talk. We at one time made some effort to require people to sit with those they did not know but we found that this did not pay. The students do not mix as much at the dinner hour as we wish they would. We see the same people sitting together too often. But they do mix a good deal, and when this happens naturally, the results are better than they were with the forced situation. If the dinner hour is to be a period of relaxation, no one should be required to open himself to more new socialization than he can take in stride. The more socialized he becomes, the less he will need the support of familiar people.

Good feeling runs high at these dinners. Groups burst into song on their own, and often the whole group is singing heartily, without a leader. Some of these after-eating song fests have been high spots for the whole semester.

To be sure, there are some who do not eat with us, but isolate themselves. Some do not like what we have to eat, or they may want to economize. Some bring their own dinners. We cannot make a profit in our objectives by trying to coerce them to join us. They are likely to join us, if left to themselves, when they hear from others that we have a good time.

We have planned social affairs. Early in the semester we take one evening session for a party. We do this on workshop time because it is as important a part of the learning process as any. It is more difficult for most of us than a regular session would be. By having it on "regular school time," many who would shun it feel more or less obligated to attend. We want them to know that we think it is important.

We have activities designed to get people acquainted. The

party is planned and carried out by volunteers from the students. Usually they are people who are having their second semester of workshop, but not always.

This party at the start is likely to be a rather stiff affair. We could have a much more pleasant one later in the semester. But the more difficult a party is, the more it is needed. The easier it is, the less it is needed. Whatever socializing value it has will aid the workshop for the whole semester if it is held early. We do this because we want to enable people to communicate throughout the semester, and not because it would be our choice as a way to spend an evening.

We usually have a social affair at the end of the semester also. This of course does not facilitate the present workshop, but by this time people have become so fond of each other that they want to play together. Those final social affairs always run off well, and everyone has a fine time.

We spend a week-end at a lake camp site. We are fortunate in Michigan in having a number of well-built camps on lakes, which can be used for conferences. To call them camps is to give something of a wrong impression, because they consist of well-built buildings that can accommodate about a hundred people, staffed by cooks, waiters, and other personnel. The camp at St. Mary's Lake, north of Battle Creek, is leased by the Michigan Education Association for use of educational groups. The State Department of Conservation has camps, notably the one at Higgins Lake, to which teacher groups are welcome. Waldenwoods, the nearest one to Detroit, is operated by a foundation.

These camps are scheduled far in advance, since the educators of Michigan believe that the camp site is the best place to hold educational meetings. There is great value in the informality of the camp. People wear outing clothes and leave their starched shirts at home. Because of the distance, people do not run in and out so much as they do when meetings are held in cities.

Each semester the workshop is invited to spend a week-end

together at one of our camps. Not all of them go. It is more expensive than staying at home, and many have family responsibilities which they cannot leave. Some few, of course, are too inhibited or too routinized to go. After getting as many members to sign up as possible, we fill the camp by inviting former workshoppers. The risk here is that we usually offend some of the latter because we cannot take all who would join us.

Thus we have a group of present members and a group of former ones. We attempt to advance the work that has been going on so far in the semester. We distribute the former members among the present ones, and let them learn from each other. The former members have a contribution to make in the area of present practice. They tell what they are doing in their classrooms to bring about the values which they have gleaned in their workshop experience.

The scene is perfect for a high social experience. The more social members of both present and past workshops are there. They are in an informal situation, where they live together— eat, work, play together. According to their testimony they get an enormous amount of work done, and have the time of their lives besides.

When they arrive on Friday afternoon, they have dinner, and then hold a planning or working session. At about 9:30 they have a recreational session. They bring to it the pent-up energy of many a teaching day. They usually start off by dancing the Hokey Pokey, which is restrained compared to what is to follow. They dance "Captain Jinks of the Horse Marines" until they are literally ready to drop. Some of these sessions where the pent-up steam is released seem almost hysteric.

As energies are spent, the tempo subsides, tapering off into ballroom dancing, and later they sit around the fireplace and sing. All of the old songs come out, as well as new ones. Communion and fellowship are at their best.

We close the conference with an evaluative session, where

the students discuss their experiences at the camp. They are unanimously agreed that it is an ideal place to work together. They soberly consider what has happened to them as persons, and what meaning the experience has for them. They usually close on a sort of solemn and dedicated note. It is doubtless true that none will ever be the same again.

The staff gives two week-ends a year to this, freely and usually at their own expense. It takes something out of them besides time and money, but it also adds to them. It is one of the big inspirational experiences of the year, and it gives the staff courage and determination when they see that people are being changed, and that this change will be reflected in their classroom behavior, to the enormous benefit of boys and girls.

The activities discussed in this chapter are our efforts to thaw people out so that they can work together. They look like play until you try them. They are essential to the modification of human beings, so that they can work on a more human level with the humans whose destiny they hold.

CHAPTER VIII

Evaluation

The problem of evaluation is a difficult one. As indicated earlier, the objectives of the workshop are different from those of the usual subject matter course. When we change our objectives, we must necessarily change the means of detecting and measuring outcomes. We cannot change our objectives and leave our evaluative methods untouched. In fact, when we change our objectives, we must also modify our methods of motivation. Motivation in most courses is closely related to evaluation. We tacitly say "I am going to make you do this, and then examine you to see whether or not you did it." This is motivation and evaluation, wrapped together in a neat and convenient package.

We believe that all teachers would be bothered by the evaluative problem if they stopped to consider what it is that they want to accomplish, and whether their evaluative techniques actually reveal whether or not they have accomplished it. But too many teachers have accepted the traditional subject matter testing ritual as valid. We, too, in the workshop, are bound to a degree by our habits, and also by the fact that little is known about methods of measuring values other than those of content. There are tons of test materials for measuring subject matter, but virtually none for measuring process or growth; almost none for use in subjective evaluation. One of the great fields in education in the next decade will be the development of evaluative techniques that will measure progress in growth, and will bring about subjective rather than objective evaluation.

These techniques will cause the learner to ask himself how he is doing, rather than cause the teacher to ask himself how the learner is doing. What the teacher thinks of the learner is of passing moment, but what the learner thinks of himself is of lasting import, because it is built into experience and modifies the organism from there on.

We think evaluation is important because it seems absurd for anyone ever to do anything without asking himself how well he did, and whether what he did worked out in the light of his unique purposes. The only place where he does not do this automatically is in school, where he knows the teacher will do it for him. Of course he evaluates even then, but not what was supposed to be learned. If he started the course to get a grade in the book, he will ask himself how well he did in getting a good grade, not what he learned.

We would be forced to think of evaluation in any event, because the workshop described here is a university course, where tuition is paid and some grade has to be recorded. The grading system of this university was constructed for and serves other objectives than the one we here set for ourselves. This is not to make value judgments on other objectives or the methods of measuring their achievement, but only to point out that we face something of a dilemma when there is no way in the university pattern for registering success in achieving our objectives. This is not the fault of anyone, but merely that whenever experimentation is undertaken, discrepancies occur in relation to over-all procedures which have been built up to serve other purposes.

Grading systems everywhere are based on competition in the acquiring and giving back of subject matter. In the workshop we are more interested in the process of learning how to work with other people than in the specifics to be learned; we are most interested in the development of human relations, of techniques of meeting and adjusting to others so that both will grow. This involves cooperation as a method of procedure.

We are of course also interested in facts learned, as long as they are pertinent to the learner. We have evidence in our evaluative material that many facts are learned, and they are retained. We believe this is due to the relationship between the facts and the needs of the learner. Genuine work is one of our chief concerns, but the work cannot be predetermined by us.

If we were to announce to the workshop that the person who showed the most growth and was the most cooperative would receive the highest grade, we would have the absurd spectacle of people competing in cooperation. The staff would have many polished apples every week. Cooperation in its true and valid sense would actually disappear.

The staff makes considerable effort to see to it that each member has the best possible opportunity to do his best. We watch for people who seem to be unable to operate well in the workshop situation, and try to give them individual help. We divide the students among us so that every student will be fairly well known to one staff member and those who seem to need individual help may receive it. We de-emphasize grades in the belief that most of the harm that comes from the grading system arises from the punitive use of them by the teacher. We never use low grades as a threat to get people to cooperate. We avoid discussion of the topic unless some student brings it up. We like to have the students feel that we are engaged in educational experimentation. If our experiment should get beyond the experimental stage and become accepted common practice, new methods of evaluation would also become commonplace.

At this point we take pleasure in giving credit to the administrators of the College of Education, Dean Waldo E. Lessenger, and the Graduate School, Dean John J. Lee, for their recognition of the fact that the standard evaluation system creates a problem when experimentation in educational methods is undertaken. They believe in experimentation, and are willing for us to fit into their system as best we can. This attitude on their part makes possible the discovery of better methods of teaching than we now know.

We do not dismiss the problem of evaluation. We work at it continuously—more so than is the case in many classes of the more traditional type. The remainder of this chapter will be devoted to a description of some of these efforts. They fall under four headings, each for a different type.

1. SELF-EVALUATION

Effort is made to cause the learner to direct his attention to his own state of mind, and his own role in the total workshop. He thinks about himself and tries to see himself, to consider whether he is doing his part as well as possible. All of our evaluative efforts have an element of self-evaluation in them, but here the learner is concerned with himself alone.

After the workshop has been in operation for about a month, we distribute blanks designed to help the student to think about his own role. These blanks are never twice the same because we try to improve them each time. Some sample questions that have been used are: What is my attitude toward workshop at this stage? Do I understand what is being attempted? To what degree have I found it possible to operate in this manner? If the workshop is not succeeding as well as it might, to what degree and in what ways is it my fault? How can I overcome whatever deficiencies I feel I have? What blocks to progress seem to lie outside my control?

When the semester is about three-fourths gone, we give out another such blank, for the same purpose, although not necessarily asking precisely the same questions. After the second blank has been filled out, we often return the first one, so that the student may get an idea concerning changes that have taken place in his attitude. The second blanks usually reveal marked changes in attitude and understanding; so much so that the student is often astonished to see what he had previously written.

This is an effort to start the student thinking about himself and his role. It is an effort to throw the responsibility for his success squarely on himself, who is, after all, the only one who can do anything about it. This is where the responsibility belongs, and we make efforts throughout the semester to place it there continuously.

2. THE SMALL-GROUP EVALUATION

Some effort is made to get the working groups to evaluate their progress as groups. This occurs mostly in two ways. The group usually has an occasional evaluative session where the members talk about how they are doing and what they need for better success. This is likely to occur spontaneously at any time, especially if there is a feeling of frustration on the part of some or all of the group members. Here they review the objectives they set for themselves and ask themselves how well they are achieving them. Blocks to better progress are identified, and ways of overcoming them are discussed. Considerable self-appraisal is inherent in this process, since it is likely to become apparent that if the group is not doing well, individuals must be responsible.

The other form in which working-group evaluation takes place is in the production of a written report at the end of the semester. This is a profitable enterprise, and the staff does what it can to bring it about without forcing it. Such a document usually starts with a written statement of the original objectives, followed by a discussion of the degree to which they have been achieved. There is usually a section on what other values have accrued to the learners from the small-group work. These often carry such items as the friendships that have been formed, the value of the social activities, the increased confidence each has in his own ability to contribute, and the increased respect he has for his colleagues.

The production of this document is a meaningful experience. It causes thinking to go on which does not otherwise occur. It gives the members of the group an additional tangible document to carry away in their hands. This stands for concrete evidence of some success in a self-motivated enterprise.

3. THE TOTAL GROUP'S OWN EVALUATION

The students and staff are of course much interested in how the workshop as a whole is meeting its objectives. There are numerous large group sessions on this subject. Not less than one-fourth of all general sessions are evaluative in nature, although they may not always be so designated.

As we go along through the semester, the planning committee is likely to plan such a session at any time. The subject always comes up because the students are naturally concerned about it and are curious about the feeling of members whom they do not know well.

These sessions usually take the form of panels, where students discuss their own feelings about the workshop and report the progress of their own groups. The discussions are broader than those concerning small-group progress because they involve all aspects of the enterprise. They discuss the effectiveness of the planning committee, the feelings they have as to the operation of the staff, attitudes toward the programs of the general sessions, social affairs, group singing, the dinner hour, the lack of facilities, and many other topics. These panels or forums are always open to the entire student body and staff. An effort is made to cause every member to feel that he has had a chance to be a part of the discussion. Not every member takes part, to be sure, for some people never get to the point where they can participate in a large group. But a large percentage does take part; it is gratifying to see how lively and interesting a discussion involving a hundred people can be when they are keenly interested in what is being talked about.

At the end of each semester, a great deal of thought and effort is put into the final total group evaluation. This is designed and managed by the planning committee, with the staff helping where it can. The last session is used for this purpose.

The planning committee usually makes some systematic effort to get something specific to talk about in this final session. Sometimes the committee gives out to each member, a week or two in advance, an evaluative sheet asking questions about the total enterprise. These sheets are collected and used as a starting point for the discussion.

Another method for accomplishing the same purpose is to form small random groups after the large group has assembled, ask that the random groups appoint spokesmen, and then devote ten or fifteen minutes to a discussion of what the semester has meant in terms of success or failure. These small groups may be formed by simply asking people who are sitting near each other to form groups. If they are sitting in rows, three in one row can turn and face three who are sitting back of them. Another method we have used is counting off. When the counting-off method is used, the groups are "more random" because people who are sitting together are separated.

After the random groups have had their allotted time, the large group is called to order. Someone has previously been designated as discussion leader. This is usually a student, although a staff member may be discussion leader if he has been asked to do so by the planning committee.

The leader then involves the whole group in an evaluative session on the entire program. It is expected that the spokesmen for the random groups will take the lead in this discussion, but not monopolize it. They make the opening remarks, but from there on anyone may speak, and many do.

In this session, there are two extremes to be avoided. One is the cut-and-dried summary reporting so common in this type of meeting. Nothing kills a meeting which has been designed to be spontaneous so quickly as a series of summary reports. People who propose this type of summary apparently believe that by hearing what went on in a group which he has not attended, one can somehow attain the status and value of having been a participant in that group. This will usually fail because there is no substitute for participation, and no one individual can be in several places at once.

The other extreme to be avoided is the final session that becomes a testimonial meeting, where each says that the workshop was wonderful. This is especially likely to occur when the semester has been unusually successful, and when there is considerable emotional content in the meeting. It may happen anyway, unless guarded against, because people in general prefer to say nice things, especially at the close. Testimonial meetings are pleasant to attend, especially for the staff, but they can scarcely be considered good evaluation.

Some of the risk of these two undesirable possibilities can be obviated by giving careful instructions to the whole group before the random groups are formed. It is possible to emphasize the fact that we really want to evaluate the semester, and that this involves pointed discussion of both the good and the bad features of it. The discussion leader, however, must have skill in keeping the discussion pointed toward really evaluative matters. This is one of the most difficult assignments of the whole course.

The final session usually constitutes the high point of the semester. Thinking which has not come out so far usually develops. Often people who have said nothing all semester come forth with pointed and intelligent comment. Evidences of growth appear which previously had not been in evidence.

The session usually ends by calling on someone to make the closing remarks. These are usually directed to the meaning of the process through which we all have gone. It is a sort of "benediction," a farewell for a time.

4. EVALUATION FOR THE BENEFIT OF THE STAFF

All of the effort in the area of evaluation so far described has been done by students, directed at themselves, their working groups, or the whole workshop. For the same reasons that the students need to look at themselves, the staff needs to ask how it is doing. All teachers need to do this whenever they teach; and they need to modify their efforts in the light of what they have learned about themselves. Universally, if half of the effort spent by teachers in evaluating students were directed to self-evaluation, teaching would be greatly improved and benefited.

Informal, personal evaluation of the work of the staff is a continuous process. There is never a staff meeting where the questions "How are we doing" and "How am I doing" do not arise. We have long discussions concerning what our role should be, and how well we are fulfilling it.

Beyond this, we need to know what the students think of us and of our enterprise. We secure information on this verbally in many ways. But we go further than this by preparing and submitting a questionnaire to the students at the end of the semester. Sometimes this questionnaire asks all manners of questions about as many features of the workshop as we can think of. At other times we have used a more generalized sheet, where we ask three or four broad questions, designed to stimulate discussion and permit generalized replies. We are usually in a dilemma as to whether or not to ask the students to sign these sheets. Some feel that people will not give their true opinions if they sign their names. Others think that no unsigned document is of any value.

We usually compromise by putting a place on the blank for signature, together with a statement that students may or may not sign them, according to the way they feel about it. Under this arrangement, about ninety per cent are usually signed; about ten per cent prefer to leave the space blank. There seems to be no correlation between the nature of the comment and the signing. One would think that if a person were full of praise for the workshop, he would sign, and that if he were most critical, he would not. Such does not seem to be the case, as some of the most critical comments are signed, while some of the others are not. It seems to be a good solution to the problem.

We have a large accumulation of these instruments, summarized, in our files. They have been collected during the entire ten years of the operation of the workshop. It is proposed here to discuss only two of them, briefly, as a detailed discussion of data would be rather boring. These two questionnaires have been singled out because they represent two different types.

The first is the instrument we used at the close of the workshop that ended in June, 1949. It is quite typical of many others. It is reproduced here in summary form. In making this summary, we have put similar statements together, and so the words used are not always the exact words of the students. To reproduce the exact words would consume many pages without adding much to the sense of what was written. We have omitted many statements which occurred only once.

Summary of Final Evaluations
Wayne University
Education Workshop
June, 1949

A. When you compare your experience in workshop with that acquired in other courses, do you feel that you have profitted by it?

More—76   Less—0   About the same—6
Comments:
  1. I have learned the techniques of democracy through actual experience. (19)
  2. I have learned to operate "under my own steam" and without pressure. (10)
  3. It has brought me out as a person. (10)
  4. I have developed new ideas and acquired new insights. (10)
  5. I have learned to understand others and get along better with them. (8)
  6. Sharing both problems and knowledge with others has been helpful. (8)
  7. This has been my best graduate course. (5)
  8. The outcomes of our group work were valuable. (4)
  9. I have learned to listen patiently. (4)

    10. I have learned to evaluate myself more intelligently. (2)
    11. I have become a better group member. (2)

B. If you were responsible for planning the next semester's workshop, will you list the methods or materials which you would emphasize more.

    1. Early social activities. (19)
    2. Knowing and using the staff. (15)
    3. General discussion at 4:30. (15)
    4. Use of library. (12)
    5. Better orientation to process. (8)
    6. Setting a definite group task. (6)
    7. More films and speakers at 4:30. (6)
    8. Knowing others outside my group. (5)
    9. More group outings. (5)
    10. Group work. (4)
    11. Continuous evaluation. (3)
    12. Eating together. (3)
    13. Defining and clarifying philosophy. (3)
    14. Techniques of workshop. (2)
    15. Bibliography for groups. (2)
    16. Rotating among groups. (2)
    17. Harmony singing. (2)
    18. Distributing experienced workshoppers. (2)
    19. Using experienced workshoppers as leaders. (2)
    20. Better room facilities. (2)
    21. General participation. (2)

Which methods or materials would you emphasize less or omit?

    1. Panel discussion. (9)
    2. Coffee hour. (7)
    3. 4:30 session. (5)
    4. Singing. (4)
    5. Concern about staff role. (4)
    6. The early workshop party. (2)
    7. Long discussions. (2)

C. Estimate the growth you feel you have made in the following areas:

Where attitude is defined as the way you feel, would you say that you have

(1) Stabilized your attitudes? Yes—33   No—21
(2) Changed attitudes?   Yes—68   No—6
(3) Acquired new attitudes   Yes—78   No—3
Are these changes
Many—37   Some—41   Few—4   None—0
When purpose is defined as doing things, would you say
that you have
(1) Done things you only
talked about before?   Yes—57 No—19
(2) Stopped doing things you used to do? Yes—55 No—15
Has your "doing" changed:
Much—25   Some—51   Little—2   None—0
Can you name one such skill?
1. Group planning with other adults. (20)
2. Teacher-pupil planning. (18)
3. Discovering pupils' interests. (10)
4. Patience with children. (9)
5. Getting children to express ideas. (7)
6. Expressing my own thoughts. (4)
7. Sensitivity to others. (4)
8. Self-evaluation. (3)
When knowledge is defined as facts acquired, would you
say that you have acquired
Much—26   Some—42   Little—13   None—0
Has this knowledge come from:
(1) Shared experiences with fellow students? (74)
Shared experiences with staff?   (58)
(2) Reading? (50)
(3) Doing?   (63)

D. Would you advise anyone to take the course next semester? (77)
Avoid the course? (0)

E. Please rate the following activities as to their value to you:

	Great	Some	Little	No
(1) Group singing	40	32	7	4
(2) Library materials	32	37	10	1
(3) Eating dinner together	61	14	6	
(4) Group work	67	11	2	

(5) The coffee period	34	31	9	6
(6) Afternoon general sessions	22	44	11	3
(7) Parties	48	24	3	2
(8) Waldenwoods	50	3		6

F. In respect to the reading you have done, how much did you profit as compared with other courses you have taken?

More—54   The same—19   Less—4

Comments:

"Am doing more reading on my own"

"Intensive but helpful"

"We bought many pamphlets"

"A list of books would help"

"Assignments from books can be learned"

"I was not stimulated to read"

G. General comments on the workshop as a whole:

1. It brought me out as a group member. (27)
2. I developed important new insights. (20)
3. Workshop narrows the gap between democratic theory and practice. (19)
4. I learned to share problems and ideas. (11)
5. It confirmed my faith in democracy. (10)
6. It enabled me to develop techniques of democracy. (10)
7. I learned that people can grow together without extrinsic pressures. (9)
8. I developed a sense of responsibility as a group member. (7)
9. I made many new friends. (6)
10. Next semester will be even better. (6)
11. I learned to be patient and tolerant with others. (6)
12. It was my most valuable course. (6)
13. I looked forward to it each week. (5)
14. I wanted to hear more from the staff. (4)
15. The staff should circulate and get better acquainted. (2)
16. We needed better group recording. (2)
17. We needed advance planning. (2)
18. It is a slow, cumbersome method of learning. (2)
19. This semester was better than the last. (2)

20. The workshop breaks down racial prejudice. (2)
21. Administrators should take it. (2)
22. We should start with a common goal. (2)

The second instrument is quite different. It is an attempt to find out what people who have been members of the workshop in previous years think about it. Here we are primarily interested in after-effects. How does the experience seem in retrospect? How has it affected attitudes, and how has this change, if any, persisted? Do workshoppers teach school differently after the experience?

In the spring of 1949 we sent such a questionnaire to all teachers who were no longer in the workshop but who had been during the past five years. Replies, then, are from people who were members between February, 1944, and January, 1949. We sent out about 450 questionnaires, and received about 150 replies. Fifty were returned because they could not be delivered. We chose an inappropriate time for sending them out, since they were received in early June, when the teachers were busy closing school or had already gone on vacation. Considering this, and taking statistical expectations into account, the return was a good one.

A summary of the results is given below. The summary is as accurate as we can make it, although the documents themselves should be seen to be fully appreciated. It took over ninety pages of single-space typing to record all of them.

A. Number of semesters in workshop
    1—51
    2—66
    3—12
    4— 3
B. If the workshop has made changes in the following, please check:
    1. Professional development—121
    2. Personal development —110
       None — 2
       No answer — 10

C. The workshop has directly influenced my teaching or administrative procedures.

Much—79   Some—53   Little—2   None—2

D. Describe practices which illustrate the influence of the workshop on your teaching or administrative procedures.

1. I am successfully using workshop methods in my classes —group work on problems selected by the pupils, planning programs, reports, bulletin boards, organizing a school congress, etc. (38)

2. I understand democratic group processes better, and I have more faith in them. (21)

3. I have changed my emphasis from subject matter and skills, as ends, to the needs of the child, individual differences, and human growth. (16)

4. I have learned to use new teaching devices. (Examples: sociometric tests, wishing well, autobiographies, seating arrangements, cooperative evaluation procedures, etc.) (14)

5. We now use group problem-solving in our planning as a faculty, and with parent groups. (12)

6. I am more understanding and tolerant of others: my children, my colleagues, my principal. (11)

7. I am better able to meet new problems. (8)

8. I am more alert to good human relations, the needs and motives of others, etc. (7)

9. I have developed more poise and self-confidence in speaking before others. (5)

10. I have learned to analyze my own techniques. (5)

11. I have more faith in myself and more courage to experiment. (5)

12. I understand teacher-pupil planning better. (4)

13. I do more professional reading. (3)

14. I have more faith in pupils and respect them more. (2)

E. In comparison with other courses I have taken, I would say the workshop was:

Less valuable—5

About the same—23

More valuable—123

F. As I recall, in the Education Workshop, I
    Did less reading than in other courses—17
    Did about the same amount of reading as in other courses—70
    Did more reading than in other courses—50

G. The reading I did in the workshop was more or less meaningful and valuable than that done in other courses:
    Much more—114   Some more—5   About the same—1
    Less—3

H. In other respects, I
    Did less work than in other courses—16
    Did about as much work as in other courses—76
    Did more work than in other courses—40

I. In my opinion, the workshop would have been better if:
  1. Better orientation to group procedure could have been provided at the beginning (lecture, pamphlet) (18)
  2. We could have more courses like workshop (16)
  3. More staff leadership in our groups (15)
  4. Better facilities (14)
  5. Better planning of the 4:30 session, perhaps as an intergroup clearing house (10)
  6. The workshop were less limited in time (8)
    Met a full year (3)
    Met two years   (3)
    Met twice a week (2)
  7. We had arrived at better group problems. (7)
    Too much stress on individual problems (3)
    Closer connection, classroom instructional planning   (2)
    Greater variety of topics   (1)
    More emphasis on teachers' organizations (1)
  8. We knew how to deal with credit-seekers (6)
  9. We could eat together (6)
 10. We could rotate from group to group (5)
 11. We had better group chairmen (or trained them in a special session) (4)
 12. We got more general participation (3)
 13. We had more speakers or films (3)
 14. We had more and better evaluations (3)
 15. We had more staff conferences (3)

16. We held more social affairs (3)
17. We had more demonstrations (2)
18. We held social affairs earlier (2)
19. We had smaller groups (2)

J. My present opinion about the workshop is different from the opinion I had at the time I was in the workshop. (38)

My present opinion about the workshop is not different from the opinion I had at the time I was in the workshop. (85)

K. Comments about my present opinion of the workshop:

1. I now believe it was my most valuable graduate course. (65)
2. I have used workshop methods and materials in my teaching. (13)
3. I have gained later insights into group process, and new values about other people. (7)

L. Summary questions—effectiveness of staff:

Too informal (3)

Some good, some not (8)

Didn't know them well (10)

Freedom of access was good (11)

Needed more help from them (25)

Helpful—enlightening, inspiring, splendid, etc. (62)

M. I would (118) would not (1) advise a fellow teacher to take the Education Workshop.

N. *Additional comments:*

I have had many courses in education, in which I have found both meaning and enjoyment, but they had little or no practical application to my own teaching situations. The very nature of the workshop process, on the other hand, brings my most pressing problems before the group for consideration.

The workshop provided me with valuable experiences. It served as a laboratory where I could discuss school problems with other teachers. Here I exchanged ideas and techniques that I immediately applied in my teaching. I always found my group interested in my results as well as their own.

Sometimes I felt there was too much idle talk about the topics without enough defining or clarification of the topics. I like the methods employed in the workshop and I feel the techniques are superior to many other classes—but often, unless a student was of the "windy" type—he was apt to be lost in the shuffle.

Learning without stress and tension was a new experience to me, and what I did learn has just spurred my curiosity on so that I have gone on learning about the things I became interested in.

The workshop has helped me to really like people. This has carried over into my classroom. I feel the most important thing to teach children is how to get along with each other.

I enjoyed the dinner hour with the group. Being table partners with colored people did more to break down racial prejudices than any other thing. I have talked and read of intercultural tolerance, but doing it was a new experience. I was extremely uncomfortable the first time I sat at a table with a member of another race as a partner, but before the end of the course I accepted it as I would any other interesting or dull companion.

I think the ideas back of the workshop are wonderful—they make the traditional courses seem stuffy and unreal. Of course the performance does not reach the heights of the theory—it never does in any learning situation, partly because of shortcomings in set up and facilities, partly because of immaturity on the part of members.

Some of the little devices used to break down personal "barriers" (such as silly games, etc.) seemed a waste of time to me. To people with more bubbling personalities, perhaps they served their purpose.

Workshop is the only class I have had where friendliness was established. I really felt that the staff cared about what we were getting. I have been able to use the knowledge, the methods I gained in workshop in my classes and homeroom. It is the first class I ever had that I got any practical help. Most courses deal in ideal situations and theories, which are very little help today because of conditions under which we work.

The greatest thing I can say about this class is that one was treated as though he were an adult—freely mature and able to use his time to the best advantage, both in class and for outside preparation. I enjoyed the contacts, the friends made, and the atmosphere.

The workshop type of course would prove valuable in other educational courses. No one could feel like shirking any amount of work if it were given like this course.

These returns show fine appreciation of the process called workshop. Of the 150 questionnaires returned, 145 were positive in their approval, 3 were mildly negative, and 2 were strongly so. Some of the statements showed that great meaning was derived from the experience.

They indicate that in a great many cases, attitudes have been changed for the better. The participants are more human as a result. They like people better than they did before. Their notions about minority groups have been changed, their understanding of the worth of all human beings enhanced.

Many of these teachers are teaching differently now. They are using workshop techniques to a greater or less degree in their own classes. They have learned to like and respect children more. They have become less punitive in their approach to children.

Because of the fact that there are those who fear that people will not do anything unless forced to, and who feel that workshop is mostly playing, we included questions as to the amount of reading and work that is involved. The returns show that most of the students did as much or more work (116 to 16), and that they did as much or more reading (120 to 17), as in other courses. They said their reading was as much or more meaningful (146 to 5) as in other courses.

Thirty-eight of them thought better of workshop, understood its meaning better, in retrospect, than they had while going through the experience. We think it is an achievement when a course grows instead of diminishing in value with the passage of time.

Every one of the principles and objectives set forth in Chapter II can be seen to have been accomplished to a greater or less degree by study of these results. It is an interesting exercise to study the results carefully and then refer to this chapter. Chapter II is the theoretical ideal, Chapter VIII shows the practical results.

Evaluation is the process through which we assume attitudes toward what we meet and what we do. In life, it is continuous and automatic. Too often in school it occurs only at examination time, and then it is more of a guessing game between teacher and learner than genuine evaluation. We need to learn how to make the evaluative process continuous and subjective. We need to work at it every time the class meets, rather than just at the end. If it is continuous, we may discover that all is not well while there is still time to do better. If it is subjective, it directs the learner's attention to his own learning and places the responsibility on the learner, where it belongs.

CHAPTER IX

Outcomes

Evaluation is the process of making value judgments on what a person is doing or on what comes within his ken. It is continuous, serving as a guide to progress. It is usually done, and best done, by the one attempting the progress. The measurement is in terms of the progress made toward the desired goal. Being a process of passing judgment on progress toward a desired objective, it should not be confused with things, such as stacks of examination papers or recorded grades. The process of evaluation is completely essential to progress.

We are not concerned in this chapter with the process of evaluation per se, but with the outcomes, which are the product of the total process. Outcomes are the differences to be observed in people as they go about their teaching and living. Not only are they what we see, but also what we feel, for the invisible change is often the most potent. This is an attempt to describe changes in personality, character, attitude, and methods of working. Outcomes are observed in informal situations, where people visit together freely. They are often matters of the spirit, the evidence of things not seen.

This is a halting and subjective invasion of an almost entirely unexplored field in education. Commonly the teacher or the administrator never asks what the actual effect of his teaching or his school has on the learner. Most academic teachers would agree that the purpose of education is to enable the student to live a fuller, more successful life as a result of his learning. But they do not evaluate in terms of this objective. They consider themselves thorough evaluators, but what they measure has nothing to do with the above objective, except perhaps accidentally. They continue to teach as they have been teaching, and as they were taught, without asking themselves what becomes of their products.

We propose here to attempt to record and describe some of the changes that have come to teachers as a result of the experiences which we call workshop. This is "unscientific" because naturally we shall discuss changes we have seen, rather than changes we have not seen. We do not believe that all students have been improved, but we see evidences of improvement in many. This will account for what may appear to be the overly positive and enthusiastic nature of this chapter. To illustrate specific points, we will give quotations from evaluative sheets illustrating various kinds of changes. These quotations could be much extended from our materials, but they are intended as illustrations only.

We justify this chapter on the ground that an educative experience should produce changes for the better in learners in order to be worth while. It is true that in some areas, notably that of general education, the changes need not be easily observable. But we believe that any educative experience in a professional school, such as a teacher-training institution, should cause an observable difference in the way in which the learner practices his profession. To be sure, no course is likely to affect practice positively in every student, but there should be evidence that this has occurred in a considerable number of cases in order to justify the existence of the course. It is doubtful that any professional course in education can be justified purely as general background, unless the learner is better able to practice his profession because of it.

1. WE SEE CHANGES IN ATTITUDES

Attitudes are all-important because they release the energy needed to translate knowledge into power. They reveal the line of unique purpose for any individual.

There is an old cliché that knowledge is power. But knowledge obviously is not power unless it can be translated into or hitched to action. Most people know many things that never relate to action—never serve them in the contriving which is life in action. There is no power in such knowledge. Action implies purpose and requires knowing (or knowledge), knowing how, and the desire to act. The desire to act lies in the realm of attitude, so that attitude serves as the release of power made possible by knowing and knowing how. Power channeled through attitude and purpose does the work that seems worth doing.

One teacher was carrying around with her a blameful attitude toward some of her children who needed glasses, could not afford them, and refused to go to the public welfare for them even when appointments were made. It was in the workshop that she learned that all welfare glasses look alike and are not like any other glasses, so that wearing them was like wearing a pauper's brand in a culture that looks down on those who need help. She was overwhelmed to learn the real reason for the children's resistance, and not a little ashamed of the attitude she had shown toward them.

A similar instance was that of the home economics teacher who was having her girls make dresses for themselves. Those whose parents could afford it brought the cloth from home, and those not able to were furnished cloth by the Red Cross. She could not understand why those working with Red Cross cloth never got their dresses done, while the others got along well. A colleague in the workshop had to explain to her that all the children knew Red Cross cloth when they saw it. One could almost literally see the scales fall from this teacher's eyes.

Changes in attitude toward fellow teachers, children, and people in general are everywhere present in former workshop students. Attitudes are probably most often mentioned in our evaluative material and in our conversations with students. Seldom do workshoppers consider any question a "fool question" because they realize that it must be important to the asker, and that a "fool question" is only one which the listener knows the answer to, although he did not always know it.

I really started thinking of the children as individuals or people, not just someone to whom I was to impart certain knowledge and skills. I have really enjoyed teaching much more and I know my children have been treated much better.*

I do not specifically do anything different because of workshop but my attitudes are more wholesome. I have more tolerance for the common annoyances of teaching, knowing most schools and systems have them. I am more understanding of my classes and more aware of what I can do for them. I am more alert for real growth and because I know I benefited from workshop where I wasn't pushed. I perhaps do more encouragement of student initiative myself.

I think it made me a more alert, more satisfied—not smug—more "searching for better methods" teacher.

My attitude with children has become less dictatorial. I found that children would work out many of their own problems if left alone with a bit of good guidance on my part, resulting in a more cooperative classroom atmosphere. I now try to stimulate children to do more selfplanning and individual thinking.

I am more tolerant and understanding of others. I have increased my mental maturity. I think and act more democratically. I have developed a more discerning mind. I have learned to substantiate my ideas. I assume responsibility more readily. I now put a different value on behavior.

2. WE OBSERVE CHANGES IN TEACHING METHOD

Reports of what students and former students are doing differently come to us continually. There is evidence of more teacher-pupil planning, better relations with children and fellow teachers, and more relaxed and less punitive methods of operation. There is evidence of greater insight into the values and purposes of other people.

* The quotations listed throughout this chapter were selected from the questionnaires received from former students (1944–1949).

A teacher recently said that she did not agree that democratic teaching was more difficult than authoritarian teaching, as is so often reported. She said that formerly she fought her students continuously, and was tense and nervous. She dreaded her teaching, and looked upon each day as an obstacle. Now that she has confidence in the general virtue of people, including her children, she has a relaxed attitude, she enjoys her work and her children, and her mental and physical health have improved.

It may be recalled that in the reports from the 1944–1949 group, 134 said that their professional development had been enhanced, while only two said that it had not.

The workshop has helped me to become a better teacher. I have had a chance to apply daily what I learned; I am better able to handle new situations; I have learned to analyze my own classroom techniques; I understand teacher-pupil planning much better.

If I were to single out one specific illustration of practices resulting from workshop experience, I would place evaluation as the most important. A sample of my own evaluation sheet for ninth-graders is included. This type of evaluation is working out much more effectively and seems more valid than any previously used.

Problems and experiences plus ideas gathered in workshop I have taken back to my own classroom and used. Not always have they been effective, but more have than not. In my classroom we have tried solving problems by group process very effectively.

Experience with the workshop gave me concrete evidence of how much can be accomplished by dividing a large group into smaller correlated ones. I put this into practice in my own situation—at best, a somewhat difficult one—and the results were gratifying. During our conference periods, particularly, we were able to get a great deal accomplished through those smaller units which undertook various pertinent school projects. We then had correlation periods at which times group reports were made to the whole class, followed by an evaluation of what we had achieved and what still had to be accomplished. This practice has resulted in a very informal classroom atmosphere, without sacrifice of self-control; the children are also reflecting a fine class spirit as a result; and they are absorbing the technique and spirit of the democratic process.

I found out that you don't have to lay down fast rules for doing things. With a little guidance children do a very good job of running a class. There are times when I found the children's ideas or methods to be more democratic than mine had been.

I have taught courses at Lawrence Institute of Technology, particularly in statistics, where I employed workshop techniques to excellent advantage.

I have had many courses in education, in which I have found both meaning and enjoyment, but they had little or no practical application to my own teaching situations. The very nature of the workshop process, on the other hand, brings my most pressing problems before the group for consideration. The workshop has been my most practical course, and the application of the workshop techniques are continuous. New problems simply challenge my pupils to participate more actively, and the results are increasingly better.

3. THERE ARE SIGNS OF PERSONAL GROWTH

A purpose of all education must be the personal growth of the individual. Teaching is primarily the business of making arrangements and affording a climate and conditions where growth may take place. This involves the development of people in such ways that they will be bigger in their understanding of other human beings, that they will be more competent to meet the vicissitudes of life.

The concept of growth calls for a new orientation toward values. Whereas we have formerly attempted to measure objectively without regard to the starting points of the various individuals, we are now called upon to observe where the individual was at the beginning and where he is now. The measurement is concerned with the change in the individual from the place where he started, rather than his accomplishment in regard to an over-all, previously established standard.

Observation from this point of view will often reveal that

what might have been considered the poorest student turns out to be the best. A number of years ago we had a student who was quite antagonistic and hostile to the entire enterprise. He paid no attention during the general sessions, and soon left his working group, spending his time in the library. He reminded us that reading and research were respectable workshop pursuits. He saw no responsibility of his own for the fact that his small group was not succeeding as well as he thought it should. Toward the end of the semester, something happened to his thinking. The accumulated experience had its effect. He said, one day, with considerable surprise in his voice, "Oh, I see! You're trying to operate in such a way that every student can profit. We never think of trying to teach any except the top ten per cent!" This and other insights which he revealed probably showed more actual growth, measured from where he started, than many of the cooperative, successful students achieved.

One evidence of growth that appears all about us is that people gain respect for their own thinking. We are schooled in the idea that what we ourselves think cannot be of much importance; that the teacher is the one who is entitled to have ideas and to express them. Before a student can be a contributor, he has to come to value his own ideas. Without this, he will never have confidence enough to put them forth. It comes as a great surprise to many of these teachers that their own ideas have value. They first put their ideas forth timidly, and slowly come to realize that they know some useful things which others do not know. When they gain respect for their own thinking, and realize that others are just about where they are, they are stimulated to think more. There is no use thinking unless your thinking has worth; conversely, feeling that it *has* worth makes more thinking sensible.

I felt that having to speak one's thoughts relevantly and coherently was hard to do at first—felt that this experience added to my personality by giving me poise in speaking before others.

As to personal development—I know I grew mentally, and I gained a confidence in using the newer methods which might have been questioned by some.

I have a different outlook on some school problems. Since taking this workshop I understand much better how to approach a problem. I also have much more confidence in myself.

By learning the group-conference method of teaching, I have been able to put this into practice in adult classes (specifically, "Sex Education for Parents" in Detroit and Highland Park schools). I feel that it was a great help to personal development because through talking to small adult groups I learned to talk to large ones. I now frequently give public lectures, which I was unable to do before.

It helped me to develop a better understanding of my pupils, their parents, and the staff at school. By sharing actual experiences with others in the workshop I learned better methods and more "tactful procedures" in my efforts in counseling. It opened new trends in my thinking and teaching, gave me new ideas not only in classroom procedure, but in helping me to aid my pupils to live better socially with others.

Having been schooled in a system where we seldom spoke unless spoken to, I felt a little lost in my first semester of workshop and saw no purpose in just "talking." I didn't realize then that in all my impatience for something to happen, more was happening to me than ever before. The associations with people in workshop have given me a very different outlook than I had before—one which has made me a much happier individual.

I have always been one of these "tense" people, always too anxious to make good grades and spent many sleepless nights cramming for exams. Then, after the exam was over, and the course finished and the grade safely tucked away to my credit, I promptly forgot most of what I had learned. Learning without that stress and tension was a new experience to me, and what I did learn has just spurred my curiosity on so that I have gone on learning about the things I became interested in. I have done a great deal of studying of my pupils and realize how little I knew before about how they think and feel.

My experience with children has not only been much more pleasant but also more effective. My experiences with parents are also happier. I only hope that I can take more workshop courses when I work on my Master's degree.

I am a more courageous visiting teacher because of having shared my problems with fellow students and staff. I have developed more self-confidence, social ability, and poise through the workshop experience.

I was pretty much fed up with teaching and its ilk. But it's a challenge every day now. To say it all came from workshop is foolish. But it started there, I know it.

Undoubtedly, the workshop was one of the most valuable and most profitable experiences of my educational training thus far. I have seen such changes wrought in personalities that I could not doubt its efficacy both in terms of changing people, which is essentially the job of education, and of producing concrete results in teaching.

I really find it difficult to express the value of the course, except that it developed my personality more than any other course, and provided a base for further growth. I think it would be valuable to have the course early in one's work for this reason. It has also developed me more as a teacher as a result of my personality growth.

4. HUMAN RELATIONS ARE IMPROVED

Changes in attitudes and feelings toward human beings as such is one of the most common and most important of our outcomes. We see people, many for the first time, sitting down with other people to meet them as humans, not just as other isolated entities. The participant has time to reorient himself to the whole business of being human among other humans. He learns to expect people to differ from him, not out of ignorance, but out of differences in what they know.

Here he comes to gain new meaning for the idea that all persons are equal. He sees equality in that all have contributions to make, all have unique experiences to contribute, all have problems which must be solved, and all are capable of spending themselves on the problems of others. The recognition of the worth of all individuals, people they have not known before, or, if knowing, have not trusted, is indeed a new insight for many. Many expressions of this discovery come to us but we can use only a few here. "I didn't know people were like that!" "I never had anything to do with people in my classes before." "I learned to like other people!" "I see the other teachers in my school differently now." These remarks bring out the essentially unsocial and unhuman nature of our educational methods, and highlight the fact that education must become a human business if people are to grow toward each other rather than apart.

I was inclined to think that the problems which arose in my teaching were only my own, but when I met with other teachers I found they were common problems and we straightened a great many of them out by using each other's suggestions.

Professionally, the democratic procedures used in the workshop classes have been invaluable to me. They never could have been learned through the usual lecture type methods used in other classes. As for personal development—I know workshop taught me this lesson: "I need my friends and they need me."

I use the workshop plan of friendliness with the parents too. While still taking workshop I planned a Mothers' Meeting (the first in the school), had all write out their names, their first one large and their last one small. We sang silly songs such as "Do Your Ears Hang Low?" and "Oh, Eliza," where you stand on "Eliza" and sit on "Jane." It established such a feeling of friendliness; I feel I accomplished more in a year than otherwise I could have done in many. When our supervisor and visiting teacher came out, I greeted them by their first names. They loved it.

I learned to work more effectively with other people. It made me more sensitive to the necessity of having a decent respect for "the opinions of mankind." It was a practical demonstration in "individual differences." I learned to like the people with whom I had to work. It gave me a new technique in group work—I have used it effectively in committee work.

I have come to understand how education in the schools has been run and I have learned how it should be run—democratically, which I have pledged myself to do. I have come to understand what important spots we teachers are in, for the good of all mankind. I have come to realize that we must cultivate the science of human relationships to the end that we may truly be free.

I have become much less dogmatic and more democratic in my work. I have been able to get students to want to achieve. I do not force them to do things they don't want to do. I have more respect for the feelings of the individual. I feel improved relations with my students.

The workshop influence has made me more aware than ever before of the value of good human relations, a deeper realization of what is most important. I have tried to get away from practices of regimentation or drill, which seemed to be a sort of an accepted procedure in our system. I can meet and talk with parents with a freedom which I had not experienced before.

The workshop has helped me to really like people. This has carried over into my classroom. I feel the most important thing to teach children is how to get along with each other.

Above all, workshop seemed to be an equalizer. Administrators enrolled in the course and on the staff whom I was hesitant to address, let alone question about their ideas, I have now curiously come to regard as colleagues. Over and over again I marvel at how a group of comparative strangers can, in one short week-end at Waldenwoods, create such a warm bond of friendship.

5. FRIENDSHIPS ARE FORMED

This outcome follows closely upon the development of better human relations. Not everyone for whom one gains new respect becomes a friend. But that human contact which causes respect is an essential step to friendship. Many of the students, through the travail of working together on difficult problems, undergoing mutually felt frustrations, and achieving a common triumph, have become intimate associates for the years that follow. It is through common action that people acquire enough in common to be able to develop a relationship that can be called friendship.

Friendship seems a pale and inadequate term for describing the relationship that follows some of these mutual endeavors. The word itself seems weak in any case, and is loosely used. What results is more in the nature of comrades-in-arms, where perils have been and are to be encountered together. While the perils are not as romantic as the dragons and monsters of old, or even the more recent dangers of the foxhole and the beach head, the risks are in many ways just as real. These comrades-in-arms have to encounter the tangles and fastnesses of old ideas and solidified concepts; to face the unreasoned opposition of a world of insecure colleagues who use all manner of devices, even ridicule, to fend the changing world which may require change of them. Comradeships formed in the human contact of mutual enterprise are invaluable in bolstering courage to act in accordance with one's new knowing.

Workshop helps to change people for the better through fellowship and gives faith and courage to cling to our ideas in educational progress in the face of reactionary factors in teaching situations.

Workshop revealed to me the need for better human relationships and aroused in me a desire to begin this work in my classes. I began in a ninth-grade social science class. After several discussions we began to develop a unit on Michigan history. We used no text but divided into groups, each group selecting that aspect which interested them most. At the end of the study we integrated it into a whole, and I felt at the end that students understood each other and their state better than formerly. In workshop I felt I gathered innumerable techniques in guidance, and in bringing students to respect themselves and other individuals' rights. I could go on enumerating the benefits received and citing examples but the space is ended so I would like to say the personal growth was the greatest received in any class, as I learned friendliness and what it really means.

The friendships formed in workshop are lasting, both among students and staff. I appreciated the real human interest in the individual.

Workshop is the only class I have had where friendliness was established. I really felt that the staff cared about what we were getting. I have been able to use the knowledge, the methods I gained in workshop, in my classes and homeroom. It is the first class I ever had where I got any practical help. Most courses deal in ideal situations and theories, which are very little help today because of conditions under which we work.

I worked as hard in my workshop course as in any other course, but the atmosphere was different. I felt anxious to be there. I enjoyed the comradeship of other people in my same profession. I made contacts and friends that I never would have made otherwise. I enjoyed the friendliness of our instructors whom I felt were "one of us." Our problems were their problems also.

6.   WE SEE PREJUDICES REDUCED

When we think of prejudice, we are likely to think of intergroup or interracial feeling. Important as this is, it is only part of the problem. A prejudice is any unreasoned feeling of antagonism toward any person or any idea. Most people carry around with them a considerable baggage of such unreasoned feelings. We have many teachers who seem to be prejudiced against people, regardless of race or creed. Others have such feelings about books, or about ideas which seem to threaten their way of life.

Such people, in working with others, learn that their feelings have been unreasoned, and that other people are pretty much like them. They learn that ideas will not hurt them—that they can be examined, and taken or left. They learn that some reading material is useful to them, and some is not; that this too may be taken or left. These discoveries cause people to become more critical of stereotypes, and more ready to judge each person or idea on the basis of worth. This is the beginning of human relations, for no such relations can exist in an atmosphere of unreasoned and stereotyped suspicion and fear.

The outcome of reduced interracial prejudice is one of the frequent and important outcomes of working together. It seems inconceivable that in a large metropolitan area we have white teachers enroll for workshop who have never had any contact with Negroes. Many times teachers have said that before workshop they had never sat at the dining table with Negroes. They think they cannot do it, but they do, and it is a revelation to them that Negroes are just like other people. By the time they have gone to the lake campsite for a weekend with Negroes, played together, slept in the same dormitories, and worked on the same problems, their unreasoned hatred and suspicion have disappeared. We have seen, and we count it a cherished outcome, prejudiced people enter the workshop and depart holding Negroes as true friends—as real comrades-in-arms.

We may have a tendency to dwell too much on the reduction of prejudice between Negro and white teachers. It is perhaps more noticeable and dramatic than the development of improved relations between other ethnic groups. The workshop has been a veritable melting pot for many such groups. Some of the groups that come to mind which have become better known and thus better liked are the Jewish, Finnish, German, Iranian, Chinese, and Philippine.

Surely the road to reduction in prejudice in any area lies in having an opportunity to really know those for whom these feelings are held. It is well known that anti-Negro prejudice is strongest among people who have never had any contact with Negroes. And it is discouraging to realize that these people know so little of Negroes that they do not know they have acute cases of a disease of serious social consequence. Once, in the early days of workshop, we invited Dr. Howard A. Lane, then of Northwestern University and recently returned from a year at Hampton Institute, to speak to the workshop on intercultural and interracial understanding. It was during the hectic months when Detroit was accumulating racial tensions which led to the inhuman race riot of 1943. We thought that in order to get as much benefit from Dr. Lane as possible, we ought to invite outside teachers to the meeting. So we called some high school principals, asking if they would announce the meeting to their faculties and invite their teachers to attend. One principal thanked us cordially and promised to do so. "But," he added, "We don't have any problem in this area because we don't have any Negro students."

We hold the reduction of prejudice between all people, and between races in particular, to be one of our important outcomes.

The association with members of various races, various schools and systems meant much to me. In fact, this exchange of ideas in class and in a social way is very wonderful.

If it had not been for the workshop I might never have become interested in attending week-end conferences where so many of the same staff people act as resource persons. I might still be a strictly traditional teacher with little understanding of the importance of respect for individual differences, abilities, and worth. I might still be interested in maintaining standards of subject matter achievement rather than in helping students to grow. I might never have had an opportunity to come to know and respect members of minority groups.

I have changed my opinion, have become more understanding, and by giving up some of my prejudices I am definitely a freer, happier person. I can think more sanely now, more logically, when I am not blocked by fear and prejudice. I'm sure I'm a more mature person. So, if I start with that, I'm sure I can do a better job of teaching. I enjoy teaching and I like people. I think the workshop techniques and methods most effective and superior to the ordinary classroom procedures.

7. WE SEE APPRECIATION FOR AND UNDERSTANDING OF DEMOCRACY

We are all committed to the democratic way of life. But our schools are basically authoritarian. We are perplexed by the dilemma of training children for democratic citizenship by giving them undemocratic experiences. It would seem that if democracy is to survive in our country, we will have to find ways of modifying our teaching techniques, and gradually replacing the autocratic educational regime. This is a requirement for the continuation of democracy in a world beset by its enemies. Learning democratic techniques is further essential for the survival of the personality of the teacher who believes in political democracy but teaches as an autocrat. Such splitting of beliefs and functions is apt, if not reconciled, to damage the teacher deeply in his personal integration. All who want political democracy and are practicing tyranny in the classroom need to note this risk.

Many of our students testify to a growth in understanding of the values of democracy and the attainment of democratic techniques that can be used in their own classrooms. Sometimes they say that it is the first educational experience where the worth of the individual was taken into account and provided for. Many say that their children are now having the benefit of democratic procedures, and that their interest has been increased through consultation, teacher-pupil planning, and activity which is in keeping with their own goals and purposes.

Since taking the workshop, I believe I have practiced more of the democratic procedure with my pupils and everyone with whom I have come in contact. The significance of training every individual for some particular type of work was made especially important to me during workshop.

From the study of democratic procedures in education workshop I gained support and encouragement for my belief in the practice of democratic principles in the classroom, even in the face of possible criticism from the teachers and principals who believe in disciplinarianism. There seems to be much criticism in most schools of teachers who, in striving for democratic situations for developing dignity and worthwhileness, seem to have less control in their classrooms which results in somewhat noisier rooms. Meeting other teachers in a truly democratic situation and finding their beliefs coincided with my own gave me encouragement to continue my efforts in democracy's behalf.

The democratic way of life could not have been taught in a more effective manner than in the workshop.

In my opinion all efforts were made to show what makes democracy click. In other words, the democratic way of thinking, working, living, teaching—all phases of democracy were taught.

The change from a vagueness in the beginning of the class to a complete understanding at the completion of the course showed that there had been much worth while growth and understanding.

Education workshop to me was a fine example of democracy-in-action. After previous conditioning as a disciplinarian it is a little difficult to accept without suspicion that the staff is not merely giving lip service to democratic procedure and that at any moment someone will "check up" and point out your shortcomings and failings. Such suspicion engenders distrust and anger until the student finally realizes the honesty of the attempt to let the group work to solve its own common problem. Many instructors, in my own past experiences, have ardently preached democracy and at the same time practiced a form of dictatorship. Living in a genuinely democratic situation and realizing its effect on myself has reassured me of the merits of practicing honest, democratic procedure which, though initially may seem fruitless, will bring lasting, worthwhile effects.

I believe in democracy, and in the schools as the chief agency of it. I believe that the schools have failed in their fullest attainment because of undemocratic administrations, much adherence to tradition, and a great lack of responsibility to the community. It is up to us to try to find a way out. I believe that if we are to have the job of making our citizens, we should be free to teach and produce free, unafraid men and women, American citizens of the highest type. We first must be free to live and work in an atmosphere of true freedom, and keep our own self-respect. When we can get this imbedded in our teachers, to the point that they can live and breathe it, know it, and recognize it at all times, then we can truly say we have arrived. Democracy in action all the time will surely bring results.

8. WE OBSERVE NEW SKILLS IN USING RESOURCES, STAFF, BOOKS, AND WRITINGS

At all educational levels, and especially in the secondary schools, colleges, and universities, teacher-student relationships are often strained and even inimical. This extends to reading material and to the process of writing. For the teacher is too often one who knows all the answers. Books are read as tedious assignments, and papers are written, not to record ideas, but to meet requirements. The accumulated attitudes of students toward teachers, which are great barriers to human relations, form an onerous cross which we teachers in higher education have to bear if we want to be human beings among humans. The barriers set up by status alone, thus automatic, stand in the way of real teaching. Patient humanness and careful avoidance of the use of status ("pulling our rank") are necessary to genuine educative achievements.

We are therefore pleased when we see evidences of a new orientation to staff on the part of students. The staff become people, with failings, with humor, with human kindness, and understanding. We see students really using staff as resources, in confidence that when they reveal their weaknesses they will not be taken advantage of. Staff become people, with only a little more experience and skill than the students themselves possess, and often lacking specific items of knowledge which students can furnish. A great teaching thrill is experienced when a staff member comes to know that he is valued for what he is—for what he can do—and not held in awe for his status.

We see students getting new pleasures out of the written

word when it is regarded as a resource, as a tool to new experience. Authors, along with staff members, lose their sanctity, and students come to know that something is not necessarily true because it has been printed. Writing for use, on the part of students, takes on new significance as they come to see that they, as well as authors, have produced the written word.

Because the teacher (as a student) was humanized in the workshop and recognized as an individual, I was eager to give the children of my class the same opportunity for expression and arrange for more democratic procedures.

I felt that the staff members were very effective. I liked the feeling that they were always available for help on specific problems and enjoyed the democratic relationships maintained. It was pleasant to know that they were interested in helping us in group or individual problems, but that they were not around checking up all the time to see whether we were tending to business. Staff members' skills in establishing warm human relationships and in improving group relationships impressed me more than any other thing.

The staff was effective in the way it stayed on the fringe, offering help usually only when it was asked, and in some instances assuming the role of student rather than authority.

The members of the staff were very understanding and very helpful so they were effective in accomplishing the purposes of workshop. I felt the staff members were genuine, sincere, and endeavoring to be helpful to us as students. There was a fine spirit of cooperation between staff members and students.

The staff plays an important part; which may be a bit contrary to one's first impression. The ability to guide without compelling and to inspire is very essential. At the same time a staff member must be careful to impart any information without implying infallibility. In other words he must be, in a sense, one of the group able to change his ideas when they are proven inadequate.

The staff must possess a combination of academic integrity and social finesse to enable them to lead through example and suggestion.

I believe the staff under this setup had a very difficult but worthwhile job to do and I feel their participation and moving about from group to group were most effective and gave us not only an opportunity to note differences in opinions but a basic belief in and respect for individuality and the rights of free expression.

I feel that the staff was well aware of their duty—not to monopolize interest groups—but to guide them when they were called upon or felt needed by the groups. In other words we resorted to books, resource people, and excursions to help solve our problems. We were not depending on the staff alone for outcomes to our particular problems.

The stiff barrier of relationship which is often accentuated between instructor and student in a formalized classroom seems outmoded to me now. The staid question-and-answer formula is frustrating. The ability to get together with others on a common problem, also knowing that the instructor will gladly help and guide, if needed, and exchange opinions, is an incentive to learn.

Because of the way our workshop is set up, with only one or a few teachers from any one school in attendance at a given time, we do not see as many changes in total school programs as we might if the workshop could involve total faculties. We can, however, point to many changes. The big change that we see is in the individual teacher, and this we hold to be the most important outcome. Programs change as people change, and people change only as they have experiences which make them see the need for change, and the ways by which they can accomplish change.

There is one small high school in this area where the entire curriculum has been modified and improved because the faculty, with only one or two exceptions, came in a body to the workshop. In one large high school the entire guidance program was planned and put into action because the principal brought a group of his teachers in for four successive semesters. In at least a dozen schools, core programs and various forms of unified studies, with extended blocks of time for students and teachers, have come about. Teacher-pupil planning has been undertaken in many instances. The enthusiasm of individual workshoppers has often spread to colleagues who have never attended, but who have seen the results of those who have.

We have had some school principals in our workshop, but not as many as we would have liked. Some who have attended show evidence of new ways of working with people. A greater influence on administration has come about by the fact that a large number of workshoppers who were teachers at the time have become principals. Most recently, a new consolidated school district has been formed, and the new superintendent is one of our most enthusiastic members. His attitudes are affecting the building program, the time schedules, the in-service teacher education program, and the basic attitudes of his teachers toward children, teaching, and the community.

Many teachers, by their individual efforts, have been able to affect whole schools, and occasionally their influence has been felt beyond their own schools. One teacher started in the workshop to study the problems of the first-grade child in learning to read. This led to a study of health and vision. She created a survey type of questionnaire in the area of vision which was taken up by her superintendent and is now used in all of the schools of that system. Another teacher, with the help of her workshop colleagues, prepared a preschool handbook for parents who have children about to start school. This handbook or modifications of it are now in use in many schools.

Such instances could be elaborated at great length. These will serve to point out that when people change, they behave differently. We can only change people on an individual basis, and they go out and perform individually. When we have better teachers and administrators, we get better results. This we hold to be the only basis upon which change can come about in a democratic society. Mass changes always have to be dictated, and are not real changes because the individual still holds his old attitudes.

The observation of intangible, but functioning, outcomes of an educative experience constitutes one of the great gratifications of teaching. These are the things of the spirit, the power which motivates action. They "must be seen to be appreciated." We see them in our present students, and in former ones. The final sessions of workshops and of week-end conferences are full of them. People reveal attitudes which make them doers. They bring renewed courage to us, and make us realize anew that what really modify people are not accumulated facts, useful as they may be, but attitudes, aspirations, and the love of mankind. These experiences give us a sort of missionary zeal for building better people through arranging circumstances for their growth.

CHAPTER X

Unsolved Problems

The preceding pages were devoted to a statement of our purposes, a description of what we do to attain them, how we attempt to evaluate what we do, and what we see as positive results. The reader may get the notion that we feel that our undertaking is a complete success, and that we have "arrived." It is true that we feel that our success has been gratifying. What the students say on the evaluation blanks, for the most part, is good. The knowledge that teachers are teaching better and that children are living better in school as a result of our efforts is a great reward.

We who see the workshop in operation know, however, that it leaves much to be desired. We see our failures, and know them better than anyone else. There are times, as we go along, when our failures and frustrations seem to outweigh the good.

Probably this is a healthy state of affairs. Nothing could be more deadly than getting to the spot where one knows all of the answers. Whenever a teacher comes to feel that he has a course organized and set up just the way he wants it, then is the time he should throw his outlines in the waste basket and begin to study his students anew. The end of problems, the end of the need for improvement, is the end of creativity. The good is often the enemy of the better. That which is held to be good will not stay good. In the stultifying atmosphere of solved problems, it will deteriorate. If it does not deteriorate, the world will move on and leave it behind.

Hence, we propose here to set forth a good many unsolved problems. These are the things we wish we knew how to do.

Many of these have vexed us throughout the entire ten years of operation, and we still do not know the answers. They leave us uneasy, contriving, and looking forward to a better semester than any we have ever known. This in spite of the fact that we know that if we ever achieved that ideal semester it would probably ruin us.

We wish we knew better ways of getting started, so that the students would have some understanding of what we are trying to do. They go through a considerable period of floundering, when communication is on a low level. They are unused to being made responsible for their own learning, and often they seek to avoid this responsibility. "Why don't they tell us what they want us to do?" "Is *this* what you want?"

This period of reorientation to the basic problems of learning is hard on the students. It is equally hard on the staff. You have heard of October's bright blue weather, but October is blue to us for a different reason. Our students have been with us just long enough by that time to become frustrated, without having had time to work their way out. The writer, for one, suffers acutely during that time, feeling every year that the workshop is possessed of an incurable disease and will never get well.

Finding that opening speeches do not have meaning and that the spoken word is fallible, we have tried panels of former students. We have even tried putting the group to work without explanation. None of these has been good. We do not know what we will try next semester, but if we can think of a new device, we will try it, since none we know serves well. Perhaps we are asking that people come to us with the experience we plan to give them, or that people were different than they are. In the face of our discouragements, however, we cannot be blamed for wishing.

We wish we could keep all students two semesters. Much of the first semester is spent in orientation. For those who do stay two semesters, the second one is always better than the first. At the close of the first semester, most students are just ready to start to reap the benefits of a new way of doing. We doubt, however, if many would enroll for an unknown quantity if they had to agree to take a whole year of it.

We do not know how to reduce barriers between people soon enough. Many students come to us with defensive attitudes, determined not to let anyone have access to their well-guarded selves. This stultifies communication, which is essential to working together. As has been set forth earlier, we use many devices for the reduction of these barriers between people, but they are not adequate. We must invent new ones, better ones.

The problem of reducing distance between staff and students is ever with us. We cannot work with people until we can become one of them. In the beginning we are regarded as teachers; we must be approached carefully. We appear to talk democratically but they have heard that before. There is an attitude of awe, built by teachers for years and years. We do achieve some reduction of this barrier, and some staff members achieve a great deal. But some of us do not, and some students come and go without ever getting over the idea that the staff members are not human beings like themselves. The load of inherited prestige or status, handed down by a long line of status-needing or status-loving teachers, is indeed heavy.

We need better techniques of knowing every student better and more quickly. When we have a group of one hundred students, there are apt to be a good many "unknowns." Nobody knows what is going on in their minds. There are ways of working at this problem, and we do work at it. But we achieve only partial success. If each student could be well known to at least one staff member by the end of the first month, many students could be helped on an individual basis to profit from the workshop. Too many students, in commenting on the effectiveness of the staff, say that they did not know the staff very well.

Although we work hard at evaluation, as is set forth in Chapter VIII, we need to learn how to do a better job. Students are unaccustomed to a self-evaluation that is continuous from the beginning, and look upon evaluation as something you do at the end of the course. When viewed as an integral part of the process, evaluation at the end is of no value in facilitating process. People need to ask themselves how they are doing while there is still time to do better. We need to start earlier, and to invent better ways and better instruments. We are inclined to forget that, because of the habits of our students, little evaluation will take place unless we induce it by showing the continuous need for it, and by showing how it can be done. We get absorbed in the machinery, and too often the first half of the semester has gone by, together with much of the opportunity to do anything about it, before we realize it. The staff itself needs to ask itself how it is doing earlier and more often. We feel that we do pretty well on the final evaluation, but not so well on the current, which can modify process. Final evaluations are the least useful, because the chance to modify action and to contrive better has gone by.

We must seek better solutions to the problem of grading. The ideal situation would be to have a hundred teachers who are in the workshop for no credit, but only for what they might learn. Since that glad day seems far away, we need to come to grips with the problem in some better way than we have done so far. We will get nowhere just blaming the grading system. It is not anyone's fault that experimentation raises a dilemma in this regard. The grading system is set up to record acquisition of content. The workshop is set up to bring about process. The grading system is unconcerned with the problem of improved practice in teaching. A student can make top grades and be a miserable teacher without inconsistency. The workshop is most interested of all in improved practices, and would like to stand or fall on whether or not those having the experience, in general, teach school better or not. We have no way of giving top grades to those who have the most democratic classrooms and the happiest children. Even if we knew how, we fear that these excellent outcomes would vanish before our eyes if we began to pit people against each other through use of comparative grade symbols. We do not even know how to determine what students are most cooperative while they are with us, or who have experienced the most growth. Perhaps some day, with the sympathetic cooperation of the administration, we will be able to arrive at a better solution of this problem than we now have. We would not want anyone to think that we are happy, or even unconcerned, about the present dilemma, or that we have ceased to think about better ways.

We have never been able to solve the problem of a good, functioning planning committee. Much of this relates to a lack of time to meet. Most of the students arrive at 4:30, and cannot get there sooner. We have tried to have a committee composed of those who could come at 3:30, thus having an hour before the general session. Often we cannot do this, and when we can, we get a committee chosen on a time basis. These members are unlikely to be representative—to be the choice of their fellows.

If we do not hold the meeting at 3:30, then it has to be held during workshop time. This takes capable members out of either the general session or the working groups. They usually meet during the dinner hour. Then they necessarily extend their meeting beyond the starting time for the small groups. This results in the committee member from each working group arriving in the middle of its session. The group often stops what it is doing to hear what their planning committee member has to report. Occasionally the group is disrupted, and never gets back to work. We are trying now to find a different and better device.

In connection with the planning committee, there is also the problem of staff help. How much help should be given the committee? Who should do it? Should one staff member meet with the committee continuously? Or should we take turns? Should they be left to themselves? Can they be expected to plan well without help when we who have been in workshop for years are still contriving?

The staff has an equally difficult problem in finding a meeting time. We do not get together nearly enough. There are six of us at present, three of whom work in outlying schools and cannot come early for a meeting. Daytime or luncheon meetings are impractical. We have tried eating dinner together, but here the time is so short that by the time we have got together and eaten our food, it is time to join the working groups. Eating together is bad practice, too, because we need to be eating with the students, this being one of our best chances to get acquainted with them.

This year we have been meeting at 9:00 P.M., after the workshop is over. This has worked fairly well. We are handicapped by the fact that we are tired at that time, and have trouble bringing fresh points of view to the discussion. We are also faced with the fact that at 10:00 P.M. the university locks the parking lots, so that we cannot get our cars out.

We feel that our students could profitably write more than they do. There is no virtue in writing for the sake of writing, but people get more out of activities if they keep records of them, and they get satisfaction from having something tangible—something which is their own—to take away with them. Further, writing causes one to be specific to a degree. In order to write about an experience, one has to think about it, organize it, put first things first. It seems desirable that small working groups make records of what they are doing, and have done; and that each member of the group have a copy to take away at the close of the group's activities. The act of doing such a common enterprise with a common product is a powerful unifying factor.

We have, of course, had a good deal of such writing, as has been mentioned under group evaluation. We would like to know how to motivate more of it, because of the value we see in it. But we know that if we make any attempt to require it, we will defeat our own purpose. We will then begin to get material written for us, instead of its being written for the writers. If the idea gets out that we like volume, fantastic phenomena will begin to occur.

We believe, then, that people who keep written records of what they planned to do, and have done, profit more than those who do not. The writing has to be done in response to a need felt by the writers in order to have much value. We are not skilled as yet in getting students to feel this need without their feeling that it must be done for us. We want to learn more about how this can be brought about within the framework of our educational beliefs.

We would also like to see more extensive use of the workshop library and of reading as a resource. While the evaluations show that the students do more reading than for most other courses, and that it is more meaningful reading, we still feel that the resource of the printed page is not fully exploited. Our students have been adversely conditioned for many years with regard to reading. They have for so long read books in response to purposes other than their own that they have to learn that the printed page is a resource and not an end in itself.

We are under the same handicaps with reading as with writing. We defeat our purpose if people read to please us. We have to learn how, much better than we now know, to get people to see that books are resources, and that they can be used to attain the students' ends.

We believe that a weekly newsletter would have a unifying effect upon the workshop. In the early days we had one. But, due to the fact that our students are in-service teachers and are with us only once a week and only while workshop is in session, we have not been able to operate one successfully. Because of the time element, most of the responsibility fell upon staff members, thus defeating a good deal of its purpose. There must be a way by which this objective could be accomplished, but we have yet to find it.

It goes without saying, perhaps, that we need better facilities, or we need to learn how to make better use of the facilities which we have. Wayne University lacks buildings, and all of us teach under great difficulties. These are multiplied when we try to do something of the size of workshop and calling for unorthodox procedures. We do not imply that the administration has not been generous in giving us such facilities as were to be had.

We particularly need a set of seminar rooms for small group meetings. Near them, we need a place for the workshop library with an adjoining reading room. One reason that more use of books is not made is because we have no convenient place for them, where students can have ready access to them. Such use as is made of them is accomplished against great odds of time and space.

We are frustrated by lack of a place to eat together. The dinner hour is an integral part of the workshop, fully as important as any other part of it. We have never solved this problem. Part of this is due to lack of facilities. Another factor has been that some want to eat little, either for financial or dietary reasons. Others, socially inhibited, have dreaded eating with strangers, and have preferred to go off by themselves or with intimate friends.

We thought that when the Student Center was completed, our problem would be solved. Unfortunately, it is worse now than it was when the building was a privately operated hotel.*

Perhaps some time some philanthropist or foundation will see the need of facilities for studying and improving methods of teaching. The view now commonly held is that sciences need special facilities but that teachers can be trained anywhere. We have been told that facilities for teacher training will probably be the last furnished, because we can use classrooms that are general to the whole university.

We suggest that a board of directors of a foundation make history by building a structure designed to enable teacher trainers to move forward in what must be recognized as being

* This need was met by the university during the fall semester, 1950.

as important as any other type of experimentation. This structure could be built to carry out the unique purposes of teacher education. It would be a recognition of the fact that if we are to have a better people, they will have to be better educated, and that the preparation of teachers to produce this better-educated people is a particular and exacting enterprise. This would be a unique departure from the idea that all one needs to prepare people for the most exacting and most human of all professions is four walls, rows of seats, and a desk.

We need better understanding on the part of our colleagues. Such understanding can only result from communication and interaction, which are lacking in college faculties. When there is misunderstanding of each other's courses, there is also likely to be criticism and a questioning attitude. Students are some-times even advised to avoid certain experiences. These actions result from our own failure to communicate our purposes and methods to the people of good will on our staff.

We cannot but feel that this is a failure on our part. We lack the facility of communication which will enable our colleagues to understand what we are doing. One reason for writing this book is the hope that many of them will read it and have a better understanding of our undertaking. It is impossible in a few minutes to make adequate explanations verbally. Most of our colleagues cannot visit the workshop because they teach at the same time. We have invited several of them to join the staff for a semester, but they all have heavy teaching loads. A single visit, even if it were possible, would reveal little.

We have a notion that if our colleagues understood what we are trying to do, we would have the support of nearly all of them. They believe, as we do, in experimentation. They believe in educative experience which is reflected in classroom practice. We need to invent new and better ways of informing them. This, we think, would result in understanding and support.

When we look back at what we were doing in 1940 and

1941, we feel that we have learned many things. Some of them were simple, but it took us as long as five years to learn them. We feel good about this progress, and we feel confident that each semester will be better than the last. We think we have learned to discard practices that do not serve, and to try new ones that may or may not work.

We think, however, that whatever progress we may be able to make, there will always be unsolved problems. They will be the challenge, the very life of each new workshop. Without unsolved problems, without a feeling of unrest because we have not done better, sterility and routine would result.

Each incoming group can feel that there is much to be done in the way of improvement, and that they will have a hand in discovering some of it. This challenges the creative genius of each group, giving zest to its contriving. The great volume of favorable evaluative evidence which we have received gives us hope that these problems can and *must* be perennially attacked (and often solved) by each succeeding group. This is what gives the workshop enterprise its lifelike quality, and it will continue to be thus as long as we can come together each year with problems that challenge our ingenuity.

CHAPTER XI

The Short Workshop

This chapter is written for those who wish to operate a short workshop, from two days to a week in length. We realize that there are few workshops that last a whole semester, and some of the procedures that have been described depend upon a somewhat lengthy experience. This method of learning applies to all people, not just to teachers. It is a basic method by which any group meeting together around a common interest can proceed.

There are many so-called workshops, in all lines of endeavor. Usually this is a misuse of the name, in our opinion. These gatherings are often completely planned in advance, and may consist largely of speeches. Even when those attending form small groups, someone is often assigned to *tell* members of the small groups about the particular topic. Often people who attend these meetings are assigned to their small groups without regard to their particular interests. The people who plan these "workshops" think that if everything is not set up in advance, the meeting will be disorganized, and nothing will happen. Even in education, preschool conferences are usually thoroughly organized beforehand, and people come to them to have something done to them, rather than to do something.

Of course we have no copyright on the word, but we would not call these gatherings workshops. They are meetings. They have no distinctive features different from the usual meeting except perhaps that a small part of the time is spent in small groups where the assignment is made in advance, and an "expert" talks to a few instead of to many. There are some essentials that we believe a workshop should have in order to have the title carry a different meaning from "meeting," "gathering," or "class."

We think that there must be a *planning session* where all are involved at the beginning.

There must be a considerable time for *work sessions* where all have an opportunity to work with others on the problems most significant to them.

There must be a *summarizing and evaluating session* at the close.

In order to accomplish all this, giving enough time to working groups to get something done, the workshop must be a minimum of two days in duration. If it is a one-day meeting, the planning and evaluative sessions will take the entire time. The working sessions give something to plan for, and something to evaluate, and therefore are the heart of the enterprise.

The short workshop will be much more successful if it can be held at a campsite, preferably away from any large city. When we have tried to operate them at hotels in large cities, attendance at the sessions is more sporadic. There are too many distractions in a city. People honestly think that while they are there they must run errands, do shopping, drop in at the office, and so on.

Another advantage of the campsite is that people are more likely to come at the beginning and stay throughout than they are in a city situation. When a group gets together primarily to listen to speakers, one may come and listen for a while and depart, but if one is involved in planning, working, and evaluating with others, he is needed throughout. There are always some who "drop in," and of course we cannot be so unfriendly as to exclude them, but we urge people to come for the whole session, and sometimes go so far as to suggest that we doubt they will derive profit from partial attendance.

Perhaps the best way to clarify the method in operating a short workshop is to describe one from its inception to its close. Not much space needs to be devoted to principles or beliefs, since they are the same as those set forth in Chapter II. Short workshops are not a product of our imagination. Hundreds of such meetings have been held in Michigan in the past ten years. Thousands of teachers have attended them one or more times. They are not related to the Wayne University Education Workshop, which has been the main consideration of this book, except incidentally, as there has been some duplication of personnel. They were started, so far as we know, by the Michigan Secondary School Curriculum Study, and have been carried on by the Department of Public Instruction, through its Curriculum Planning Committee and subcommittees. They are discussed here as illustrations of short workshops, and not because they have much to do with the major thesis of this book.

On the very day that these words are being written, there is such a conference in progress at St. Mary's Lake Camp, just north of Battle Creek. This camp is leased and operated by the Michigan Education Association. It is in use throughout the year. It is so much in demand that plans and reservations have to be made a year in advance. The workshop now going on is sponsored by the subcommittee on Secondary Education of the Curriculum Planning Committee. Its topic is the Core Curriculum, and its membership is made up of teachers who are either teaching some form of Core or are planning to do so. There are one hundred and eighty reservations. This is the more remarkable because the conference starts on Friday morning, so all of these teachers are there on a school day. Their administrators have arranged for them to be away, are employing substitutes to take their classes, and in most cases are paying their expenses.

A description of what is going on may be the best way to tell how a short workshop can be operated.

There had to be some preplanning. This is always true, but a crucial question is what kind of preplanning should be done. The conference had to be conceived by someone (in this case the committee on Secondary Education), and a reservation secured. The conference had to be advertised, and someone had to be responsible for receiving the reservations. A temporary chairman was chosen, who is responsible for opening the first meeting and carrying the conference on through the problem-finding process until the planning committee of participants could be formed and take over. The temporary chairman needs to secure some help in carrying out the problem-finding process from those who had had experience in it. The preplanners may want to secure a recreation leader in advance, or they may decide to depend upon talent which is always to be found in such a group.

This is just about all of the preplanning that needs to be done. To do more than this may tend to prevent the development of growth of the conference group through participation in planning.

The conference will open with a few songs, as a means of setting the tone of the conference. Then one of the preplanners, or someone they designate, will probably make a few opening remarks. This is a brief welcome, and a statement of the objectives of the conference. The person chosen for this should be someone who can get it done in a maximum of ten minutes. Care should be taken to see to it that no long-winded speaker ever be chosen to make the opening remarks.

Then the temporary chairman with his helpers starts the problem-finding process. It is shorter than the one described in Chapter III, but the principles are the same. There are many variations of the method, but we shall describe a representative one which usually succeeds. The total group is broken into small groups by counting off. The small groups are instructed to appoint recorders, and to make a list of the specific problems on which the members would like to work. Forty-five minutes should be enough time for this to be done.

The total group is then reassembled, and the recorders report the problems proposed by their groups. These problems are listed on a blackboard, with similar ideas being consolidated, so that there will be as few topics as possible. Then the members are asked to choose the topic in which they are most interested. Thus we have formed interest groups.

When the interest groups meet, each group is asked to choose a chairman, a recorder, and a representative for the planning committee. Then each interest group goes to work on its problem. Since the groups will not be together long at best, they will probably not be able to define their objectives sharply, but most of their work for the conference will consist of exchanging ideas on the particular problem which has brought them together.

Soon after the members of the planning committee have been chosen, they get together to plan the rest of the conference. They choose a chairman, and he or she replaces the temporary chairman who had been appointed by the preplanning committee. The permanent chairman is therefore a person chosen by the representatives of the participants. He has emerged from the group.

The planning committee, after its organization is over, proceeds to plan the rest of the conference, deciding how much time will be allowed the working groups, what use is to be made of the rest of the time, and what devices will be used for summarizing, evaluating, and closing the conference. Their plan is submitted to the whole group for criticism, and also by each representative to his small group. If there is any strong or general criticism of the plan, the planning committee will need to reconsider it, making modifications on the basis of the desires expressed by the group.

In any such conference, there will be a certain number of resource people. They are people who have come not only as learners, but to help with the conference. If none make reservations, the preplanning group may need to invite some. In Michigan, however, with its considerable experience in this type of education, there are almost always enough resource people who come without special invitation. Many who came originally to participate as members have emerged as resource people. All are potential resource persons, and we try to reduce the importance of specialists, so that new leadership will continuously emerge.

When the working groups are meeting, some care should be taken to see that the resource people are well distributed among the groups. Some member of the preplanning group should attend to this. The function of the resource person, or "staff member," is primarily that of one who can contribute ideas and who knows where helpful materials may be found. He needs skill in helping others to discuss, and needs to know when to keep still. The main risk in this situation is that he may take charge of the group, talk too much, stifle others, and prevent the contributions of others being made.

In the evening, after the work is over, some thought needs to be given to recreation. The people who most dislike recreation need it most. Tonight at St. Mary's, someone will probably lead the group in a grand march, which will be followed by the Hokey Pokey and Captain Jinks. There will be square dancing, the Virginia Reel, and many others. Most of those present will participate to some degree, the length of time depending on the condition of their arteries. At about eleven o'clock, there will be a snack, probably sandwiches and coffee. After that, a group will form around the fireplace, and all the old songs will be sung again. Those who go to these conferences expecting long and restful sleep are unlikely to achieve their goal, because they will become involved and forget it.

These recreational activities, which are so important to the success of the conference, may occur spontaneously, but it is best to do some planning, at least for part of it, to get it started. In the Core conference going on today, it will probably start by itself.

The final session, an important part of the workshop, will be planned by the planning committee. The committee needs to concentrate on values, rather than specific details. An open discussion on what the group has gained is usually interesting and worth while. The planning committee may ask someone to make a final closing statement. This is a good idea because it brings the meeting to a close without dwindling to an end, and it enables each to leave the meeting on a positive note. Persons who are inclined to attempt to summarize or who have poor terminal facilities should be eschewed for this assignment.

The people who participate in these two-day conferences or workshops usually leave in high morale. They get a lift from having lived, played, and worked with those who are engaged in the same kind of work, who have the same types of problems, but who seldom get a chance to share their burdens. Often there is a sort of spiritual quality to the communion that has taken place, and this causes a rededication to ideals that tend to become latent when one works alone. People often leave these meetings with enthusiasm for the business of being human and seeing their jobs as human jobs. We do not understand all that happens to people when they fully share. We often wonder how they can get so much for so little. We value the enthusiasm, the renewed courage, the spiritual uplift that accompanies the actual facts learned by the process. This attitude is what translates the knowledge into power.

We realize that a continuing group process is more difficult than these short workshops. The latter are together for so short a time that they do not go far enough to get into trouble. In the Education Workshop, they come to the point in their work where, if they have not planned well, their process breaks down with a resultant loss of morale. This will also happen in a week-long conference, but is unlikely to occur in a two-day one. Perhaps all this means is that for the two-day workshop to be a success, it is not necessary that those present be experienced or skillful in group-process techniques.

Let us see what has been done when a short session has been operated on a workshop basis:

1. The subject matter of the conference has been derived from the learners.

2. The participants have had a chance to operate in accordance with their own purposes.

3. Each member has had a chance to contribute; none has needed to remain passive.

4. Leadership has had an opportunity to emerge from the group, with the consent of those led.

5. Each has had a chance to engage in doing, rather than being cast in an inactive, listening role.

6. Fundamental human needs—a task, a goal, and freedom to move toward it—have been provided for.

7. Barriers between people, which prevent communication, have been reduced.

If you are planning a two-day conference, the following guideposts may be helpful:

1. Do only the minimum preplanning necessary to get the people there and to get started.

2. Depend upon the needs and interests of the participants for your program.

3. Avoid long speeches, particularly by people who are chosen for "name" reasons. Most such persons do not know much about the problems around which the conference is called.

4. Secure a place where continuous attendance will be encouraged.

5. Stake your success upon the willingness, ingenuity, and creativeness of the general run of those likely to attend.

All too few preplanners are able to take a chance on the success of such a conference. Past experience has created barriers to such thinking. They are unaccustomed to programs that are not carefully planned in every detail far in advance. They fear that performance will be sloppy unless they take steps in advance to prevent it. They may think that nothing will happen unless they make it happen. They presuppose that they know the needs of the group, without having seen it. This feeling is doubtless the product of our educational conditioning, where the teacher provides the program and naturally thinks there would not otherwise be one.

It does take courage, especially the first time, to depend upon the general effectiveness of all people to know best how to go about solving their own problems. It takes courage, while not surrendering a feeling of responsibility, to stake one's reputation for responsibility on the faith that others will come through. It takes vision to see that the best way to carry responsibility is to give it to others. The reward of this faith in others and willingness to gamble on it is great.

This whole book is oriented to teachers and their education. This chapter is appended in the belief that the method of learning that has been developed with teachers is equally applicable to all kinds of people who assemble for the purpose of learning. Teachers do not learn differently from other people. They have, however, more adverse conditioning to this way of learning than other people.

We believe therefore that the method of learning here described is as useful to conferences of lay people as it is to teachers. We feel sure that businessmen, labor groups, farmers, plumbers, school board members, musicians, or any other group can best learn together by taking responsibility for their own learning, and that they can learn more from each other than from any expert who may speak to them. And so we commend this method to all who would meet and learn.

CHAPTER XII
Conclusion

This closing chapter takes the form of a conversation between four people who have read the foregoing chapters, and who are familiar with the Wayne University Education Workshop and with similar techniques used in other places. The conversation was taken by a tape recorder around a fireplace at Waldenwoods during a spring camp experience. Some of the participants wanted the author to be present to help them point up their remarks. Believing that responsibility should reside with the learners, he declined. The remarks have hardly been changed. They are substantially as they were poured into the recorder. It is worth noting that they are centered on the promise of the techniques for learning, rather than on the details of the manuscript.

The four participants are Roland C. Faunce, Associate Professor of Secondary Education at Wayne University and a member of the workshop staff for four years; George L. Miller, Director of Admissions at Wayne and a staff member for twelve years; Marie I. Rasey, Professor of Educational Psychology at Wayne and a staff member for ten years; and Fred G. Walcott, Associate Professor of English Education at the University of Michigan, teacher at the University High School, former chairman of the Curriculum Planning Committee of the Michigan Department of Public Instruction, and a veteran of many workshops and conferences both at the University of Michigan and throughout the state.

FAUNCE: Now we four have read a book that reports a new kind of teacher education, an experimental approach to teacher education, which is different from conventional programs. It represents in many ways a different set of values than are commonly sought in teacher education and it reports many significantly different kinds of products or outcomes from what we have come to expect in conventional programs of teacher education. I wonder if we four would like to comment on what those differences are as we see them. In what way does this represent anything that we can capitalize on?

WALCOTT: I think the differences are fairly represented by the difficulties that the author and his associates have encountered in workshop operation. The responses that he complains about are those that are developed by traditional types of education, are inherent in those types of education, and are bound to accrue as long as those types are fostered.

FAUNCE: What would you say, Fred, were the significant elements that you refer to among these values?

WALCOTT: Well, one is what we might call a universal timidity on the part of students, a disposition to take on a protective coloring by silence, to avoid hazarding a voluntary statement that may bring ridicule. Another is the competitive instinct that is manifested in the disposition of some few students in the classroom to monopolize, to do all the talking, while the majority sit back secretly scornful but silent. Then, there is the common inability to work together cooperatively, to hold significant conversations on points at issue, the inability to ask pertinent questions, the inability to make helpful suggestions to a person who is making a statement. All of these things together constitute a general inability in cooperative communication. I think that these are all symptoms that every one of us recognizes in a typical classroom, maintained in the traditional manner; these are the obstacles that one encounters in the beginnings of the workshop: and it is these things that have to be replaced with new dispositions.

RASEY: That seems to me to be one of the strong points in this book and one that would be particularly helpful. I think it is not only the timidity of the student to hazard a guess at something. That timidity is the natural end product of common educational practice. Our older education seems to have been tacitly built upon the idea that the director of the class knows something which it would be a good plan if the members of the class knew, and an attempt is made literally to transfer it through the air. By the process described here, when students are oriented to the idea of learning from each other and by experience, they begin to have confidence in their own thinking. Then, therefore, they are automatically more willing to express themselves and that is partly due also, it seems to me, to the fact that we all tend to operate in terms of configurations to which we are accustomed. Older education offered us a question-and-answer type of method. Great caution was required on the students' part that the answer be right. With so much emphasis on right answers, the more veiled they could be, the better bet it was that what the student said would pass. In this book I am so glad to see that we have a clarification of some techniques, some devices and tricks in the trade, that can replace the methods of dealing with students that are less true to our facts.

FAUNCE: There are two things in this approach that impress me and strike me as significant, and I know these are not the only ones that we will think of. But it seems to me that reflected all through this story is the tremendous concern on the part of the so-called professors and instructors for bringing about desirable changes in human behavior on the part of participants, as individuals; for making a more constructive, more courageous people as opposed to the conventional goal of hacking away at a certain body of subject content which can then be given out at appropriate terminal points. The other is the concern for group relationships which seems to be accented all through this story, which I am sure we will all agree is a true emphasis in terms of what we know about how the workshop operates. Do you folks think those are important differences between this approach and conventional course structure?

RASEY: It seems to me to be a very important point. While it is definitely labeled and geared towards a workshop practice, it has great usefulness for other types of classes. The thing that impresses me is that if one undertakes to reorient his teaching in his own classroom in terms of human relations instead of subject matter there are no patterns, or at least few established patterns, for undertaking to do so. We have a dozen patterns for trying to transmit a body of information from one person to the other persons. Now if a person undertakes change in his own classroom, when no workshop condition is set up, he can find a great deal in these procedures here described with which to modify his own behavior in his own group, in his own classroom. That ought to be a lot of help to all of us.

FAUNCE: Does that seem to imply that there might be a carryover into teaching, as one chapter in this report indicates —a considerable amount of transfer into actual teaching procedures in the behavior of a teacher with the youngsters? What would you say about that, George?

MILLER: Yes, I think that there is a significant amount of carryover from workshop into actual teaching procedures. As experiences are accumulated and evaluated teachers in the workshop begin to find other goals than the acquisition of subject matter. Attitudes and skills in working together become important. Each one learns what it feels like to be a part of a group. Contributions of each member are respected. The teacher behaves differently. This cooperative behavior is carried over into the classroom. They have learned that it is easy to acquire an answer and that behavior patterns develop somewhat more slowly but the growth process is more natural.

WALCOTT: Well, I am a little inclined to differ with you, George. I don't believe that human beings are inclined to be slow to change behavior patterns if they can enter a different climate from the one they are used to.

RASEY: I agree with that—that is right.

WALCOTT: I think traditional education constitutes a climate that is, itself, conducive to behavior patterns that will persist as long as students remain in that climate or imagine that they are in it. The moment you interview students in your position, on the prospect of entering the University, they immediately assume that the climate they are entering is the same as that they have left; and as long as they believe this, they are going to continue the same behavior patterns pretty much. The fact is, they can't imagine the kind of climate described in this book, and they can't see themselves operating in a new climate they can't even imagine. Now, if you could translate them into this new climate, I think you would discover that their behavior patterns would change fairly rapidly. We have plenty of evidence of that in past workshops. People develop an immense cooperative ability in the progress of one semester, and those who take more than one semester of a workshop make astounding gains in their ability to work constructively with others. I believe that this kind of education is natural—that is, it conforms to the nature of human beings and their inherent drive to learn by doing. It is exactly the kind of activity that the learning infant employs. It is investigative, it is cooperative, it uses the people and the things in the environment. Children do this spontaneously. It is only when they enter school, with its traditional climate, that they lose these facilities.

FAUNCE: Shall I tell a favorite story of mine and a true one, Fred? It illustrates your point about using human resources. Perhaps based on the notion that one of the first things they learn, and you say they learn it with rapidity, is a new point of view about other folks. We had a workshop member who confessed to us after the first week or two of her relationship with her group, "This, I find, is an unusual group; this is a better than average group of teachers I am in. I am so glad I chose this group." A little later she had a chance to meet with other workshoppers and to visit other groups and at the end of the semester she said, "You know, I discovered when I got into the other groups that they too were a better than average group of teachers. I have come to the conclusion that ninety per cent of the teachers are better than average." This may be poor mathematics, but excellent psychology and good pedagogy because she has made a significant forward stride, I think, in her view about other people. She is ready to believe now not only that they are good but that they can be helpful to her, that she needs them, and that interdependence is basic—that she has also started to think about her role in helping others.

WALCOTT: Now I am convinced that despite the advantages of the traditional education that we have all known—and those advantages are numerous—there is something in it that is also stultifying to human beings—that is, it blocks learning in the natural way. An example comes to my mind from my own field, English. I am thinking about the research on the practical value of English grammar, on its efficacy in changing the patterns of speech and writing. The research on that problem is more than forty years old. Every bit of that research is negative. I know of no evidence whatsoever that a knowledge of grammar has any effect upon the way the possessors speak or write. I am sure that that research has been reported in methods courses, in textbooks on psychology. I, myself read it years ago in Starch's old psychology; and yet whenever I go to a meeting of English teachers and mention those facts, they seem to be completely astounded; they cannot believe that it is true. They come forward with all the stock rationalizations to prove that it isn't true. They say things like this: "Well, what are we going to do? The colleges are expecting this kind of training. How are children going to succeed in college if we don't give them this training?" They completely overlook the point at issue, the fact that such training doesn't prepare for college or for life. Can you tell me how a great professional group like that, made up of people who have gone through colleges and universities and have been teaching for several years, could get into that state of mind, could be ignorant of the very research that their educational institutions have tried to impart to them, or could ignore it if they have encountered it? How does it happen?

FAUNCE: Is it possible that how we feel is more important than what we know, and indeed conditions what we are ready to know?

WALCOTT: I think that that is true, but also, assuming that it is true, it seems to demonstrate the point that I was making a while ago; that despite its virtues there is something also stultifying in traditional education—it produces the wrong feelings in us.

FAUNCE: You are going to react to that, Marie?

RASEY: We have had that verification in so many cases in workshop. We are all committed to the statement of fact that you can't transmit by word of mouth, that individuals have to learn by experience, have to have something on which to have the word take root. Yet let us get into a crisis where the method doesn't seem to be going right, instead of working harder with it, we are very likely to fall back on our old ways which we know aren't right. We do some more telling and plan an introductory lecture.

WALCOTT: You mean the teacher does this?

RASEY: Yes. In our workshop, for instance, we have done this repeatedly. It didn't get under way fast enough to suit any of us so we tried one device after the other and they were all cut off the same pattern practically. That was that somebody must try to say it more succinctly, so that surely these people were going to hear it, and then at the end of the semester with exactly the same speech repeated, the students would say, "Why didn't you tell us that in the beginning?" They couldn't hear it until they had experienced it. It seems to me there is a lag in catching our practice up to the scientific facts we know to be true in every area of our teaching. It is not only in the teaching of technical grammar. I have thought that the difficulty lay in the imaging. It isn't quite imagining.

It is the problem of imaging what is to take place. We can't conceive, for instance, that one's tongue could twist more accurately around certain sequences of words unless he had studied rules. That is the way we have been doing it. It must be right. Yet there isn't anybody who doesn't know that a tongue learns to twist by twisting and not by dealing with the abstract rules. This seems to me to be one of the over-all difficulties and I think that this book clarifies some of those issues, so that I feel I could do a better job in classes that I am responsible for myself, out of the evidence that is presented here.

FAUNCE: I think English teachers, and indeed all kinds of teachers, have got to feel comfortable and secure and respect themselves in the techniques they use in the classroom. Now something is missing somewhere along the line that produces this lag between what we know in the research sense and what we know in the functional sense of being able to do it. I think English teachers do what Fred complains of—and this isn't confined to English teachers—because they feel more comfortable doing what they themselves have mastered after many years; and they haven't developed that same kind of security in some other approach in language education.

It takes us back to the same point that how you feel, especially toward kids, especially toward other people in general, is more important than what you know intellectually. You have to feel comfortable and you have to feel secure, and the workshop has a valid contribution to make in that regard. I have thought a number of times that after a semester or year of the education workshop a kind of by-product that is clearly evident to me in these people is a liberalizing of their views toward functional education; something which we haven't sought to do as staff members, completely a by-product and resulting I think from a greater feeling of comfort, security, etc., in interaction with others. After a semester or year of workshop they are more ready to accept a shocking idea such as Fred reports from the research. Now is that wishful thinking, in your opinion?

MILLER: Isn't there evidence of that in looking back over some of our experiences? Last night one of the problems that was raised in the group was that of subject matter. Where does it take its place, what are we going to do about it? It seems to me that in most cases it is the individual who is new to the workshop who is always concerned about subject matter. Isn't there evidence that after proper attitudes, security, and the feeling of sharing experiences is realized, this brings about liberalization? They no longer harp on subject matter alone.

RASEY: Something else comes into that too, I think, and that is what seems to me to be a natural tendency on the part of all of us to think apathetically when we are in any new area or when we have been shocked by anything. You so often hear this said, "What do you mean, you don't care whether they read or you don't care whether they can do arithmetic?" As though centering something on human relations obviated one's knowing any of the tools of human intercourse. When this thing happens, and people become a little more secure in their own thinking and more securely critical of their teacher's thinking, it seems to me they can occupy themselves with middle ground instead of reckoning with the fact that if you are going to talk about human relations then it means that you don't care anything about subject matter. I don't think people can see middle ground, can see moderation, until they have recovered from the first shock of an apathetic point of view.

FAUNCE: Maybe courage is the product of interaction. They draw strength from each other and they learn how to do that in the workshop. Is that a point?

RASEY: I think so, and with the competitive aspect which has been so central to our education for so long there is no security. Every other student is an enemy until you have proved he is your friend. From this angle we proceed as though all people were friends, all people were equally able to assist each other. This makes for much confidence.

WALCOTT: I think that point needs enlargement. It is an important one. Thinking again of this insecurity that many people manifest everywhere in competitive life, I can't help believing that traditional education is pretty much responsible for it. The position of the learner in traditional education is a subordinate one. That is, he is required to obey, he is required to follow directions, he is required to do assignments, he is required to do someone else's work, he is required to act in the way someone else approves. He grows up under traditional education in the presence of suppressive authority. His condition is that of a slave; he takes on the temperament of a slave, the submission to authority to the extent that he has to, or to the extent that it is meanly expedient. His rebellions are usually of a sly, secretive nature. As a matter of fact, the more admirable forms of rebellion, those that are overt and outright—forthright, I would call them—are usually considered the most reprehensible of all.

FAUNCE: In school you mean?

WALCOTT: Yes, that is right. Now, students under those conditions develop all of the slavish traits, and I think some of the outstanding ones are insecurity, lack of self-respect, lack of confidence in the presence of other people, lack of ability to cooperate with others in common projects; and I suspect that right there is just the condition—or at least these are the antecedents of the condition—that you are describing when you say that teachers feel insecure.

RASEY: I have some evidence in that direction about written work in classes. It took me a long time to surrender my supposed prerogative to assign papers. I ask the students to take the first few weeks and discover what they think it would pay them to expend themselves on this semester, and then choose a field. In the beginning they say: "I thought I would do so and so, do you think that will be all right?" And when I say again, "What would make it all right?" they are in confusion for a time about what would make it all right. It is reiterated that if it will serve you, then that would make it all right and no one else but you would know. Toward the middle or the end of the semester you may have somebody coming up and saying, "I got interested in so and so, and I asked my kids what they thought about so and so and it is very interesting." "What do you think about it" takes the place of "Will it be all right." It seems to me of necessity that this growth is slower than the mere regurgitations of fixed answers. So there appears to be a slower process in that kind of growth because a person has really to reorient himself completely in the thinking of what the objectives are. Actually the difference is between growth, slow or fast, and no growth.

WALCOTT: We are all plagued by that kind of thing. I invariably try to suggest permissive activities to students—take composition, for example. It is unthinkable to me that people cannot find something within them that is worth expressing and that they ought to want to express. But when I talk to them about seeking their own inspiration, they will invariably come to me when they have an opportunity and say, "How long do you want this to be." Or, "Would you suggest a topic for me to write on?"—things like that, which indicate again the slavish dependence on someone to give them permission and make their decisions.

RASEY: And the inability to conceive that you would value *their* decision.

WALCOTT: That's right.

MILLER: Those remarks remind me of Dr. Dybwad.* The speaker said the real threat in the world to peace and co-operation is the structure of the German family. That is, the real threat is not necessarily Communism, but authoritarianism. He described the structure of the family with the father as the head and the rest of them as, quote Fred, "slaves"—a complete authority that no one questions. He goes on to

* Dr. Gunnar Dybwad, Director of Child Welfare, in an address before the Southeastern Michigan Roundtable, in Ypsilanti on May 6, 1950.

describe the conditions which existed previous to World War II during which time they were involved in a completely authoritative educational pattern. No action, no participation, no decisions were made by these people. When hundreds of thousands were cremated, no voice protested. When asked why, they shrug their shoulders and say they have no responsibility in the matter. You see, there is no feeling that they are a part of it. You illustrated this when you told about the student coming up and saying, "How many words has this got to be." Under strict authority people do not participate and decide, they only follow.

WALCOTT: They have no responsibility to rebel or to protest.

MILLER: That's right. Now then, to go back to this English teacher, or anyone of them in the various areas, aren't they in that same niche so to speak? Instead of taking advantage of what we now know from research, to see if they can improve their teaching, they simply shrug their shoulders and say, "Well, we are doing what we are told to do." In other words there is that line of authority which has followed down through their experience. Maybe that explains some of the confusion when we open up workshop. Everybody's looking for that authority, and as we experience workshop, cooperative participation develops. People become responsible.

WALCOTT: I think that habit of thought is illustrated over and over again in the excuses teachers frequently make—they are really rationalizations. They so often say, "Well, we can't do this unless we get the approval of our principal," or "Why shouldn't this kind of thing start from the top?" "Why shouldn't the superintendent start this thing and give it sanction?—then we can do something." They seldom assume that they themselves are a prime authority, that they too have a responsibility to suggest and to initiate. There is a protective hierarchy, which they really prefer to submit to.

FAUNCE: George, you have been a member of the workshop staff since the beginning, haven't you?

MILLER: Yes, we started it.

FAUNCE: I suppose nowhere in the country is there a single teacher education workshop that has operated for as long as twelve consecutive years. I was wondering whether you could see any change in that regard. You mention the initial confusion and the seeking for an authoritarian role for the staff, a dependency, an irresponsibility. I have about become resigned to the assumption that we shall always be confronted with that and have to work around it and that the only way in which people can learn is through experiencing that initial chaos or confusion. I was wondering, though, whether in twelve years, the confusion has been ameliorated? Is it any better than it was a dozen years ago, or not? Or have we learned any techniques through our experiences?

MILLER: Oh yes, I think we have learned a considerable number of techniques. The process has changed considerably from what it used to be. The whole structure of the workshop, when it started, followed the line of authority pretty well. The director was a director and everyone in the workshop looked for and got direction as to the type of problem and the areas to be studied. For example, our afternoon periods were always cluttered up with visiting firemen or some local individual who would come in and tell; it was a telling process; when we broke up into smaller groups, groups were assigned to staff members who were definitely staff in the sense that they were faculty.

WALCOTT: Then they represented a certain area, didn't they?

MILLER: They represented a certain area very definitely. As a matter of fact that is how you grouped the people—around the staff person.

WALCOTT: That is my experience from the beginning.

MILLER: That's right. Now then, we no longer do that. For example, the role of the workshop staff is a participant and we try as nearly as we can in that role to help them as resource persons along with the other resources that we have in the group. We pool our thinking and from that we draw conclusions as to how we can move forward or what we want to do about the things that concern us. There is another thing that I think I see that has been a definite change. At no one time in the earlier periods did any of the students ever assume responsibilities of planning what they wanted to do or take responsibility upon themselves to be participating members. They were just there to hear. I am sure that we have learned how to get away from that role as staff members and I am sure that in what we are doing now there are more evidences of people joining, becoming a part of the gang, and playing their roles, sometimes as resource persons, sometimes as leaders, and sometimes as followers. There was none of that evidence in the beginning at all.

FAUNCE: And where else but in the workshop—well, this is too broad a statement but I'll make it anyway for the emphasis—where else but in this kind of an approach, at least, do you have individual students worrying, or groups of students worrying, about the welfare of somebody else in the course? Now when you get that, I think you have got hold of something fairly significant in terms of the values Fred was talking about.

MILLER: I don't know whether this follows your conversation but there is another thing in which I see a definite change. In the afternoon sessions, the speakers involved—the people who were telling—rarely had any connection with the immediate concerns of the people. They were interesting, they were people who had specialized in certain fields. It didn't make any difference whether or not we needed it; we got it. At least now we are trying to make those 4:30 sessions functional and an opportunity to explore and help the groups and the individuals.

RASEY: I can see out of my ten years' experience with this group, I think, one type of change that is manifested in three separate areas. This one George speaks about is among them. It seems to me we had a vestigial remain—somebody talking who represented an authority, papers that had to be written and books that had to be read. In the early semesters we were much concerned with speakers. We tried to find some way by which we could guarantee an articulation between what the speakers said in the afternoon and what some of our groups were working on in the evening. We got into awful messes trying to make those things hitch. Then we were greatly concerned for fear we had not a considerable item of writing for every student in the file every semester. I can remember that in bridging that thing we practically required that a student would at least put in a paper that said he had been concerned with a certain area. If it did not make itself into a paper it made itself into a sheet to be on record for him. We operated in the first place with our remarkable library trying to get the books nearer to the students. We built bookcases on wheels to take the books into the various groups. I think we did this without any conscious realization at the beginning, at least I did not have any, that books would not be used, no matter how much you made students fall over them, out of any mechanical answers we made to it like the bookshelves. It would only be when the students found out that there were between covers of books things which they themselves wished to know, not something that some professors required them to get. It seems to me as we have moved our emphasis off of those three shelves that we have had all the things come to the fore which were really liked. We have more and more talk in the afternoon which comes from the people who are right now wrestling with these problems and they are the problems which arise in the small group sessions.

WALCOTT: I am glad you made that point. There is an important aspect of "authority," in quotes, that I think we ought to recognize clearly in education; and when I use *authority* in that sense, I mean the learning or the ability that any person has acquired in any area. That kind of authority is important; it is useful to man—it can be—and the whole point of its usefulness seems to me to depend on whether it is sought for a specific purpose, not imposed or poured in because the authority sees fit to do so.

RASEY: Might it not be almost parallel to the way most of us behave about advice?

WALCOTT: Right.

RASEY: If we have a problem and seek out someone that we believe knows more than we do about it we hang on his words. If somebody comes and gives us advice that is unsought, we are offended.

WALCOTT: And that is one of the most important things for us to keep in mind. Even little children do that. It is the most natural thing in human life to ask someone who knows, to ask for help, to ask for advice, to ask for sources. There is another point mentioned earlier that goes right along with this line of thinking. I am referring to the use of the term "subject matter." I am very sensitive about comments on the term, because so often I find educators disparaging subject matter and talking in terms of teaching the child or teaching the human being; and I know that when they say that, their sentiments are right; but I don't believe that anything that man has thought or learned or written or done in the world is unimportant. But, of course, it is too vast a fund of knowledge for any one person to do more than sample, and I think that the importance of that vast record of man's thinking and doing depends again, as authority does, upon whether or not it is sought. I am completely confident that if we develop this workshop type of education, we should give eventually a new respectability to subject matter of all kinds. That is, we can replace the common negative attitudes of stultified learners by the simple desire to seek and to find, to increase and to utilize.

RASEY: I have been amazed among graduate students, where most of my work lies, how difficult it is for a graduate student to get hold of the idea that he might be using a book for some purpose of his own; that he is always concerned with what it is that you want him to get out of it and does **not** recognize that he can get out only in terms of what he brings to put into the hollow words. I remember one student said to me, "Did I understand you rightly? You said you did not care whether we read the books or not." I answered that I had no personal interest in it. He asked: "And I don't have to write any book reviews or cards?" I said, "No, I have read the books I recommend and I should think your writing ought to be in terms of what you want for your own reference." He said, "Do you realize that we could cheat?" And I said, "I think I also realize whom you cheat." He was a blond fellow and his face went red clear up into his hair. He said, "You win." It apparently was an embarrassing concept to him.

MILLER: This reminds me of some experiences we had when we were working on a cooperative program in a junior high school. The school was concerned about subject matter and we were concerned about meeting the needs of young people. First of all we established good morale by discussing ourselves and our needs on a cooperative basis. We planned our work together and adjusted it as we sat down from time to time for appraisal. The interesting part of it was that the youngsters acquired more, and more functional, subject matter. In other words the knowledge that they were seeking became a part of them and they were using it because they wanted to get at it. They were getting answers. In checking these youngsters, for instance, in American heritage or the background of American life in the contemporary picture, we found that students in our group did not know all the same answers as those who followed the usual pattern of the textbook but they had a better understanding, and could talk more intelligently about issues and trends and movements, and the behaviors of people in our country than the others. The amount of reading, for instance, they did in seeking answers was far greater than in the usual class. This curiosity broadened them far beyond the usual pattern where authority would have stifled it.

RASEY: I wondered a lot about that, George, and I wonder if it isn't due to the fact that when the people are learning in this fashion they are learning psychologically instead of logically. Textbooks are put up logically but there is inherent in that logic a comprehensive overview on the part of the author, whereas we all learn from our interested question, moving to a pertinent answer.

MILLER: That's right.

RASEY: For everybody, that's different.

FAUNCE: You know, I have been thinking as I sat here, why it is that we have such high morale, and I think we do. There is a good bit of evidence that we have high morale in this workshop, semester after semester, especially toward the end of the experience. By way of getting at that question I asked myself why I look forward to the workshop, each week, with anticipation that's really high. I don't want to miss—if I do miss the workshop I do it with the greatest reluctance and wonder what went on. When the time approaches I go over there with high hopes and anticipation. Why do I do that?

I have come to the conclusion that I have two feelings about the workshop. The first is a feeling of warmth; I am going to join some friends toward whom I feel very warm. I haven't seen many of them for a week and I am anticipating it as a rich experience. It is a friendly, warm, permissive, congenial kind of atmosphere, and so I look forward to it. The other reason I think (and perhaps these feelings are shared by participants), the other feeling I have is that it is an exciting, experimental kind of an experience. I think, as I go to the workshop, something is going to happen today. I don't know what it is but it may change me—may change my professional thinking—indeed it may change my life. It is an anticipatory kind of feeling that I have. Now these two feelings affect whatever techniques, whatever methods, as reported in this book, are used as we continue to sharpen our approach and try out the new methods. I hope we will be able to retain those two values because to me they are very important.

MILLER: The workshop and these experiences which we have at Waldenwoods and Clear Lake and St. Mary's are really the same patterns only in different places. One of the things that has been quite beneficial to me and I am pretty sure it is the same for a good many other people, is that I know more about myself. I know more about my own behavior because I have been sharing viewpoints and it is this sincerity, this friendship, this exchange, which helps me to clarify myself and see myself much better.

WALCOTT: What you folks are saying is, in substance, that we have here a natural pattern of learning, a natural pattern of human relationships; and I think there is a lot of encouragement to be found in the curiosity that young people have for this kind of thing. I find that my students are surprisingly eager to find out more about it. Young students of education are wanting to know where they could get a position that would allow them to work in the "Core," which, to their minds, means this kind of cooperative planning and discovering objectives and carrying them out. I believe that this is probably the most significant thing that has happened in higher education in our time, and I believe that is one of the reasons that this is going to be a very significant book.

Index